REAL FRIENDS

REAL FRIENDS

Becoming the Friend You'd Like to Have

////////////////

Barbara B. Varenhorst

C. Gilbert Wrenn, Consulting Editor

HarperSanFrancisco
A Division of HarperCollinsPublishers

FIRST EDITION

Designed by Catherine Hopkins
Chapter opening photographs by John Lund

Library of Congress Cataloging in Publication Data
Varenhorst, Barbara.
  REAL FRIENDS.
  Bibliography: p. 193
  Summary: A handbook on peer counseling teaching the skills of building friendship and reaching out to others who are lonely, shy, disabled, and especially in need of friends.
  1. Interpersonal relations—Juvenile literature.   2. Friendship—Juvenile literature.   3. Youth—Juvenile literature.   4. Peer group counseling of students—Juvenile literature.   [1. Friendship.   2. Interpersonal relations]   I. Title.
HM132.V36   1983   158'.25   82–48412
  ISBN 0–06–250890–3

92 93 94 95 MPC 20 19 18 17 16 15 14

Contents

Preface   *vii*

1. Turning Someone into a Zero   *3*
2. I Said Hello—And You Know What Happened?   *21*
3. What Do You Ask?   *41*
4. What Do You Hear?   *55*
5. Come, Lonely One—Welcome   *71*
6. What Do I Do After I've Listened?   *93*
7. The Me I Am Now and the Person I Am Becoming   *117*
8. It's Hard to Say Good-bye   *141*
9. Priceless Gifts from Real Friends   *163*
10. Peer Counseling: Teaching How to Become a Real Friend   *181*

Acknowledgments   *192*

Books on Counseling and Human Relations   *193*

Index   *195*

To the memory of my nephew,
David Oak Ebright

Preface

- How many *real* friends do you think you have—friends who have shown in many different ways that they care about you?
- How many people do you know who will take the time to listen to you without judging or advising, hearing beneath the surface of the words the feelings you have?
- Which of your friends do you talk to about important, personal things like what you hope to be doing in the future, your fears about going into high school, or your problems in getting along with your dad?

How many people do you think consider *you* to be that kind of real friend? Are you someone who knows how to help another; who can be trusted; who doesn't use another to get into the "right" group; who brings out the best in people you meet and come to know? Is it important to you to become a real friend—the kind of friend you want to have? You may even long to become that kind of friend to yourself.

When you are lonely, troubled, depressed, or down on yourself, there is nothing as precious as knowing you have a friend who faithfully and genuinely cares about you. Even when you are happy or proud, you need a friend who wants to hear about it, who will give a hug or a slap on the back to say, "You're okay!" Friends like that are priceless, because real friendship cannot be demanded or purchased. It must be *given*—unconditionally, just because someone cares. Everyone wants that kind of friendship, and many want to be that kind of friend. But often a desire is not enough. Sometimes you have to learn how to act on that desire—learn the skills of how to care about others.

Learning how to become a real friend to oneself and to others is what is taught to young people in a program called Peer Counseling. The idea for the program came from listening to students talk and noticing how they treated one another. As a former junior high teacher and counselor, I often saw how much my students needed friends and yet how cruel they were to each other. In talking to me, they admitted that they wanted to act differently; they wanted to be kind; they wanted to be able to help their friends— but they didn't know what to do. How could they change? How could they learn to help their friends?

Realizing their desire and need, with the help of school district friends and Dr. Beatrix Hamburg, a former Stanford child psychiatrist, I started the Palo Alto (California) School District Peer Counseling Program in 1970. Student reaction to the idea is summed up in a comment one student made when she heard the program was starting. "All of us kids knew that we turned to our friends for help, but we never expected an adult to realize that too."

Over the years since the program was started many students between grades 7 and 12 have been taught how to become a real friend, as well as being given the opportunity to use those skills to reach out to lonely, shy classmates. Some have given their friendship to students who are physically or mentally handicapped, others to members of their own families. Many have learned how to become a friend to themselves.

Other school districts, churches, mental health agencies, and even correctional institutions across the country have initiated similar programs. Most of these programs are for adolescents. But the idea has expanded now to adult populations, including caring skills training in churches, training in hospitals for cancer patients who have had radiation treatment, and even senior citizens' peer counseling programs.

Despite all this activity, many young people still have not had a chance to be involved in such a program or be exposed to the friendship skills instruction. Knowing this, I felt a need to share what is taught to peer counselors in such a way that it would be helpful to anyone, but particularly to young people who have not had an opportunity to participate in peer counseling. In addition, by my use of illustrations and details from my work, I hope to stimulate readers who are new to this idea to become interested in finding out more, or even in starting similar programs.

It was important to me to write this book for young people. Many other books have been written for adults, as self-help instruction or as guides to becoming more effective in working with adolescents and children. I wanted this to be a book *young people* would read and use, particularly as they are going through that period of their lives when they are very self-critical, extremely sensitive and vulnerable to peer influence and pressure. In using narratives, anecdotes, and occasionally the actual words of students, I have tried to stimulate excitement about what can happen when young people are assisted in developing the positive idealism that is within most of them.

My "story" about caring and friendship begins with what I see happening to today's youth, and why many young people feel like a nothing—a zero. Most of the remainder of the book is devoted to teaching how this can be changed—how society can become more caring and how people can learn to care about others and become real friends to those who need a friend. The story ends with examples from the lives of students and some adults illustrating the power of caring and how it has changed their lives, as well as those of others. In some instances throughout this book, names of individuals and other aspects of the examples are changed. The last chapter is written for those who want more specific details of what is involved in implementing a peer counseling program.

The book is obviously written from my bias as a psychologist who cares about people, who thinks that each person is important as a person, and who has a religious faith that supports these convictions. Many of the great religions of the world testify that love and concern for others is very important. In the Christian faith, Jesus placed such importance on our relationships with others that he gave us a commandment to love our neighbor as ourself. I believe both youth and adults desire to fulfill that commandment. But often we are confused about what this means in terms of thoughts and actions in everyday living. The caring and friendship I am describing is one that *reaches out* to others, putting aside self-centeredness; that is a concrete caring for *individuals* rather than a vague love for humanity; and that is a caring that is *motivated toward action* rather than an armchair emotional feeling. These are the threads that are interwoven through each chapter.

Real Friends is also a thank-you to the many students who have become my real friends, as well as teaching me and providing valuable assistance, and to the adults who have made peer counseling a reality. Each of you has taught me much about caring—about myself and others. As you have helped shape my thinking, you have become part of the story. But much of the story still is left to be written— by you the readers, irrespective of your age, by putting into practice even in small ways what I have tried to say and teach in writing this book.

REAL FRIENDS

Turning Someone into a Zero

The thin fifteen-year-old boy with sunken eyes, wearing faded jeans, silently goes in the school door in the morning and comes out the school door in the afternoon, and that is all. Sitting in a back seat in the corner of his classroom, he stares into space, unnoticed and unimportant. Eating alone at lunch, nibbling at his sandwich, he watches his classmates playing ball on the field; he is excluded from the laughing, whispered, intimate conversations, uninvited into the group. Neither smiling nor talking, he sits alone on the bus that drops him off at the road that leads to his house. Day after day, the faces and the voices say, "You're a nothing, Cliff Evans." And finally he goes away on a cold April morning and dies on a snowbank.

Jean Mizer's poignant, true story of Cliff Evans in *Cipher in the Snow* rips the heart and shocks the mind. In disbelief that this could happen to a quiet, gentle boy, the mind protests: This must be an isolated case—a stark, unusual tragedy!

But is it? Open your heart and look around you. Do you see

JERRY, the tall slim boy with the long hair who is a physics "brain"? He lives alone with his father and stepmother, who are never at home because they are involved with their own professional lives. He always seems tied up when you try to talk to him, so the words don't come out right. You have to really work at trying to find something to say to him—so why bother?

YVONNE, who is fat and pigeon-toed? You probably don't really know her because she always goes home for lunch. If she didn't, she would be sitting alone, not having anyone to talk to or spend time with when classes are not in session.

MARK, who mumbles a lot and tries to get your attention by reviewing all his problems? But you never take him seriously, and it's so easy to ignore whatever he's trying to say.

RITA, who has the terrible scar on her face and who often sits silently looking out with that vacant, dejected look on her face? Occasionally you and your friends may laugh at her— but she doesn't even seem to notice. She lives in a world of her own.

You don't dislike these people, because they don't mean that much to you. You don't particularly want to hurt them—because they are "nothing" to you. They know it. They hear it. And the feeling of worth and value they have for themselves goes down.

Perhaps you can understand why, when you think about it. Obvious put-downs or ridicule are very cruel, but at least the person who gets treated this way knows he or she is a person who is noticed. It is the unintended slight or exclusion, or not even being aware you are present, that really cuts away at your sense of worth. When no one needs you, notices you, or even looks at you, you no longer need, listen to, or value yourself. If this continues, gradually you emotionally die.

Some of you may know how this feels. Perhaps you think of yourself as a "nobody." Maybe you think you're the only one who feels this way. Not true! In 1973, a survey was done with junior high school students in Palo Alto, California. One-third of the students reported that they felt unnoticed or unknown by peers and teachers. Some said they had no contact with anyone during a day other than by being present in a classroom. Others felt the school could care less if they didn't show up each day. Maybe Cliff Evans would have said some of these things if he had been asked to complete that questionnaire. These are the feelings and conditions that make people feel as though they are a zero. Sadly, this feeling is present everywhere.

Young people aren't the only victims. Many adults also feel they are unimportant to anyone. But it is more painful when you are young, because adolescence normally is a self-critical period of life, no matter what you've got going for you. During this period of your life, you are struggling with everything: yourself, your family, your energy, your appetite. You question your abilities, appearance, and worth. This is normal. But society has created some conditions that make it even harder for you to arrive at adulthood as a healthy, self-responsible human being. These conditions are what I am calling the unnatural "handicaps" of adolescence. Before I explain them, I want to talk about what one student called the bumps of adolescence—what I consider to be the normal difficulties of this period of your life.

THE "BUMPS" OF ADOLESCENCE

Students were sitting around talking about what each had learned from being in peer counseling. "Peer counseling helped me smooth over the bumps of adolescence," Debbie shared. "What *are* the bumps of adolescence?" Linda anxiously asked. Knowing she was two years younger than Debbie, Linda was worried about what she had ahead of her.

The bumps to Debbie were rough periods with her parents and friends, slight bruises that had healed partly through time, partly through the understanding she had gained about herself and others in her peer counseling class. For Alan, the bumps were getting his height and physical stature later than his peers. Having to wear braces for two years affected Tammi, and being flat-chested all through high school made Shirley miserable. For Kathy, the rough times were not over, as she continued to experience her parents' suspicions and distrust, making it hard for her to feel good about herself.

Most young people live through these bumps and eventually get over them—or even forget them. But some bumps leave emotional scars that are never forgotten, which make some people vulnerable to certain pain at any time of their life. You may wonder why some can emerge from adolescence almost unscarred and why some are deeply hurt. Why are some people sturdy emotionally and others so fragile?

Perhaps part of the answer to the difference is the kind of support you get during adolescence when you experience these bumps. Some of you have parents who *do* understand what is happening to you. They are patient, helping you to adjust with understanding and love. Many of you do have friends who are able to help, who like you despite your braces, lack of muscles, or undeveloped breasts. But some of you don't have this kind of support—or at least enough of it. You may be laughed at, left out, or made to feel inadequate because you aren't coordinated, beautifully developed, or as cheerful as you used to be. When this happens, the bump may turn into a wound that is never quite healed.

THE HANDICAPS OF ADOLESCENCE

Even if you are one who has been fortunate enough to have help getting over the bumps of adolescence, you still face some obstacles that affect all young people living in society today. These obstacles are the "handicaps" that have developed as society gradually has changed. These handicaps are

- **the tendency of adults to hold a negative bias toward young people: *The Problem-Prone Image* handicap**

- few, if any, meaningful contacts or relationships with adults: *The Separate Worlds* handicap
- decreasing opportunities to contribute to the world in general and to help others in particular: *The Closed Door* handicap

As I explain why I think these are handicaps, I want you to think how they are affecting you. As you do, however, remember that you don't have to be defeated by a handicap. You *can* do something about them; the rest of this book attempts to suggest what you can do so that when you enter adulthood you will feel you are a somebody, rather than a nothing.

Handicap #1. The Problem-Prone Image

A young person is like a jigsaw puzzle in which the pieces never seem to match. You charm and terrify. One day you're vivacious and the next depressed; one moment you're kind and in a flash, cruel. At times you are helpful, but often indifferent. Some of you are popular, but many of you are lonely. Some of you work hard to achieve, but too many of you are afraid to risk possible failure. You can be poised and confident or awkward and scared. Some of you value your life, and others want to throw it away.

Being around a living kaleidoscope isn't easy. It takes a lot of energy, patience, and even faith to wait until the beautiful butterfly emerges from the not-so-beautiful cocoon you are breaking out of. Lacking the patience or understanding, we adults, unfortunately, concentrate on the negatives of youthful growth and behavior. We even play them up and publicize them. As a result, we tend to expect that all young people will get into trouble or create problems.

With these odds against you, it's a pretty hefty challenge to think of yourself as a good, desirable, or worthy person. As Merton Strommen writes in *Bridging the Gap:*

When a person enters his teen years he inherits a public image that is distorted and negative—one that pre-conditions adult attitudes. Youth find this image reflected in the chance remarks of some adults, in the articles or pictures of mass media, and by the ways in which people in authority treat them. To most youth the negative image is an obvious fact; to most adults it is not so apparent. (p. 12.)

John is a high school student who knows from personal experience how this negative image hurts:

John had been chosen to be one of the students to attend the peer counseling workshop in his area sponsored by drug and alcohol prevention funds. The workshop was held in the new county facilities and those working there referred to the sessions as the "drug school." When John went home at the end of the first day, he was eager to tell his mother what he had done and learned. As he began, however, rather than being interested in what he was saying, his mother sniffed around him suspiciously to see if he had been smoking pot. When she found he hadn't been smoking, she walked away in disinterest. Hurt, John went to his room and turned on the TV for companionship—feeling a little less of a person because of what his mother had expected and done.

Images or reputations aren't created by accident. They usually are based on some reality. Probably John's mother knew he had smoked pot many times before. Now it might take repeated evidence of his not smoking to change his mother's expectation. Changing a negative image to a positive one is difficult, but it can be done. Here's one good example of how some young people have done it:

When I began exploring the idea of starting a peer counseling program in Palo Alto, many adults were skeptical, if not outright critical. They were *sure* adolescents would not be responsible, interested, or willing to do anything unless they got out of class, were paid, or got credit for the training and work they would do. This meant it was going to take dramatic evidence to change their minds. The training was scheduled after school, on the student's own time, at a centrally located training center, which meant students had to get there by their own means. No credit or pay was given for the training, and students had to make up any sessions they missed before they could be 'credentialed' as peer counselors.

To the astonishment of my adult critics, 150 students met these commitments and fully completed the training. As most of these students volunteered to continue as active peer counselors—*on their own time*—adults heard the message! By the third year of the program's activity, teachers and administrators were asking for peer counselors to help with significant problems. Clearly, these peer counselors had helped to impress the adult community *positively*, chipping away some of the original negative image adults had expressed.

But you have another group to convince, and here it will require the work of each one of you. The fear and problem expectation associated with youth has filtered down into your own feelings about your classmates. When you are with your peers, many of you anticipate cruel treatment rather than kindness; ridicule, rather than understanding; evaluation, rather than acceptance. This means that each one of you carries a heavy responsibility for helping or hindering a classmate coming to feel like a nothing—or like a happy, more secure *person*. Overcoming the handicap of a negative image of youth, among youth themselves, can only be done by you. It can be done—*if* you want to, and *if* you learn how to be a caring person.

It is sad that we don't need instruction in how to hurt another, but we do in how to care for others. This is true because everyone has been hurt at some time in his or her life. That experience teaches how to be unkind. But not everyone, apparently, has experienced sincere caring and love. It is hard to be kind, accepting, and loving if you've never had any models for it or experienced what it is like in a relationship.

Most parents and teachers *do* care, but even some of them don't know what to do to show how much they really care. Some confuse being responsible for you with caring about you. There is a difference! Responsibility means a willingness to be accountable for what happens to you. Caring means being involved, being concerned about what happens to you, being interested in having you grow and develop as a person. A caring person has eyes that see a multitude of things and ears that hear even the silence of the silent. Caring expects the best of a person, caring with the heart as well as the mind. Caring forgives and allows you to start over again. Caring sees you as an individual—not a stereotyped image.

So, maybe you feel too many adults only feel responsible for you—and very few care about you or even *like* you. But feelings work both ways. Do you *really* care about them? What do you suppose would happen if each of you began to show more care and love to the adults in your life? This might make a dramatic change in how your parents or teachers feel or think about all young people. If you don't know how to go about it, learn how! Then start teaching how to be a caring person to others, beginning with your parents. I know enough of you would be willing to do this, because you're tired of the negative attitudes people have about youth and you're sick of how your friends and classmates treat one another. You don't want to end up being a cipher when you're an adult, and you don't want this to happen to others, either.

Handicap #2. The Broken Connection Between Separate Worlds

If you are now in middle school or high school, you probably are spending a lot of time with friends in your own age group, not only for companionship, but also to learn how to act socially and to find out what people are like, as well as exploring who you are or want to be. When you're with your friends you talk about problems, play together, imitate one another, share secrets, compare physical development, and complain about your teachers. It seems friends are more understanding. They know more about what's happening to you than adults and have similar problems or painful experiences.

But friends may be no more able to give you help than you are to help them. They are uncertain, too. They may not admit it, but often your friends are confused or scared about what to do. So you really do need adults as a backup; as people to turn to for help who have had more experience, a broader perspective, and even sometimes more wisdom. You also need as models some adults you respect, who provide you with ideas about the kind of adult you want to become. Young people who have a close, warm, trusting friendship or relationship with a mother, father, aunt, teacher, employer, find that it has shaped their thinking about life—their goals and purposes. However, for this to happen, a young person has to want it, and adults have to be available and willing to get involved in that young person's life.

Take an inventory of the adults in your life—parents, grandparents, aunts, uncles, teachers, neighbors, family friends. Which ones of these people do you feel you really know and do you feel are close to you? Which ones have influenced you in your thinking about yourself or about life? Which ones would you like to know better? What stands in the way of this happening?

We don't do anything together. Diaries and records that children and youth have kept give clues to some reasons. It was found in studying these records that few children spent as much as two hours a day with an adult other than a teacher; that few meals were eaten together as a family. When children were not in school they spent most of their time alone or with peers, mostly watching television, eating snacks, or "fooling around." Although some went shopping with their mothers, almost none did errands or chores or contributed in any other way to the running of the home. Rarely did a child work with an adult on some project or even observe an adult at his or her work.

There's no time to be together. Three hundred seventh- and eighth-grade boys were asked to keep records of the amount of time they actually spent with their fathers over a two-week period. Most of these boys only saw their fathers at the dinner table, whereas a sizable number did not see them for days at a time. The average time a father and son were alone together for an entire week was seven and a half minutes! Obviously some must not have seen their fathers at all for this to be the average total for the group.

You don't make the effort. A meaningful relationship can't be built, help can't be received or given, if you don't have the opportunity or time to be with your parents. It's not just their fault, however. Maybe *you* haven't tried to make an effort to be around your parents, or maybe you're not too pleasant to be around when the family does do something together. If you want more meaningful time with a parent, you could turn off the TV and offer to help with dinner. As you worked together, maybe you could talk. Without being phony, try to get your mom and dad to talk about their work—not just about what they do, but how they feel about it. If you asked your dad or mother to teach you to play golf, you could join one of them on Saturdays. The same applies to any sport. Or why not take the risk and offer to teach them *your* favorite game or sport? Another way you could snatch some conversation is helping your dad or mom do the grocery shopping—either going to and from or while waiting in the checkout line. Even remembering to ask your parents about their friends can open a conversation. If your interest is genuine, it says loudly that you want to be involved. As you *model* what you want from a relationship

with your family or other adults, you may find them following your example in how they react to you.

These suggestions won't always work or produce over-
night the relationships you may want or need with adults.
Parents—all of us adults—have to change and make an effort also. We have to give some sober thought to our priori-
ties and how unskillful we often are in relating to young
people. But until this happens, your peer group may be
your lifeline. If you don't have a group, as Cliff Evans
didn't, it can be damaging. But even if you do, surviving in
the world of your peer group can be pretty difficult, especially if you are cut off from any adult to assist you.

What's It Like in That World of Your Peers?

I don't have to tell you what it is like in the peer groups
you're connected to or you deal with almost every day of
your life. You know better than I do. It isn't all helpfulness
and sharing. There is an ugly, cruel side of these groups that
can't be denied. I know this from listening to students.
What I have heard are put-downs and feelings of loneliness,
confusion, rejection, and inadequacy because of what classmates have said or done. This means that adolescent groups
deserve much of the blame for why many young people
feel like zeros. Would you agree?

Let's go into some of the details. When most groups of
students talk, they eventually get on the topic of cliques.
They suffer from them, they wish they didn't exist, and
they perpetuate them. In the flow of discussion, individuals
become labels—the "burnout," the "jock," the "brain,"
"street-wise," "cowboy," and under one name or another,
the "loser." The label "identifies" the group, and some
groups seem fair game for ridicule and laughter. Some students don't matter enough to even have a label. No one
knows their name! As cruel as some labels are, they may be
better than being nobody to anyone.

What does all this do to how young people feel about

themselves? In 1970, 7,050 high school students, randomly selected to be surveyed, talked about their feelings. What they said was presented and explained in the book *Five Cries of Youth*, by Merton Strommen. I recommend you read this book, but I want you to at least hear about some of the students' feelings.

One out of five of these students reported feelings of worthlessness, self-criticism, and loneliness. The critical issue was the need to have friends. Most who felt this way said that outside their families they really belonged to no group and were bothered to some degree by their lack of friends at school. Tragically, a few harbor thoughts of severe self-criticism and even suicide. A small number said their loss of contact with themselves and others is compounded by a feeling that even God does not care about them.

We can't just shrug our shoulders and say "too bad" when we read such information. We have to do something about it—and we can! The details of what we can do are explained throughout this book, beginning with the next chapter.

How Can the Adult World Help?

The help you and your classmates want or need differs depending on who you are. Some young people don't want any help. But if you were given a list of forty possibilities of things that might help you improve your self-confidence and feeling of importance, it's likely you'd find some of your requests on the list. The students in the *Five Cries* survey were given just such a list.

Two items were chosen by the largest number (78 percent). These were *to find meaning in life*; and *to learn how to make friends and be a friend*. Almost as many chose opportunities that involve leaving their public posture and taking off their masks: *I want to be more of the real me in a group; I want help in finding friends and learning to be friends to members of both sexes; I want to be part of a caring accepting group.* Two-thirds want a group whose members, in addition to offering one another acceptance, also confront one another with honest, frank sharing of personal feelings. Others checked that they wanted to find ways of dealing with their lack of self-confidence and want assistance in understanding themselves and the reasons for their problems.

Can a peer group alone provide this kind of help, especially when each person in the group has the same or similar needs? Your own age group will always be important to you, but when you are an adolescent, it may not be sufficient. Without healthy contacts with some adults, you may be greatly handicapped in your attempts to value yourself—and then to value others.

Handicap #3. The Closed Door to Usefulness

A third handicap you face as a young person today is in your search for ways to be useful and needed, ways to add to the world rather than just to be a taker. How can you become a valued team member in the work and life of the world you live in? What talents or abilities do you think you have that are now being used in meaningful activities? What talents do you want to develop so you can make a contribution in the future? What is one thing you have done that makes you feel worthwhile?

There was a time when it would have been ridiculous to ask young people such questions. Everyone knew he or she was needed and why. Youth had chores to do, they contributed to the family farm or the city business. Then, gradually, this changed. Young people no longer were needed as much in the work or the economy of family and community. As this happened, many were deprived of the natural ways of learning to become adults. Now, often denied even a paying part-time job, many young people can't pay for their own gas or supply their own spending money. This has robbed many of you of respect from your families and respect for yourselves. Too often you are seen as economic burdens—and some of you are expensive to maintain!

No one, youth or adult, enjoys being a burden. If you are deprived of ways of contributing financially or of doing any other socially useful task, where does this leave you? It leaves you, first, unprepared for independence as an adult, and second, with a low image of self-worth. Such negative feelings of personal worth may explain some of the increase in suicides of youth. In the *Five Cries* study, Strommen found that after loneliness, the clearest evidence of a low self-regard was thoughts of self-destruction. You do have to have a *reason* for life to be precious. You are more likely to feel this way if you feel useful to someone.

I'm not saying that there is no work to be done or nothing that young people can do. Sometimes you miss real opportunities because you feel you aren't good at anything. This is not true—of anyone. It is frustrating to hear so many of you say it, though, especially because some of you believe it. Your doubts sometimes come from not having had many experiences of feeling successful or of achieving things that give you pride. Everyone remembers failures; some also forget successes. What people remember, they use to predict or imagine what will happen in the future. Young people have no problem remembering what they consider to be failures. But some are hard pressed to come up with what they remember as being successes. Many then imagine that their whole lives will continue to be unsuccessful.

Getting good grades and being active in athletics are the most common ways students get recognition. Grades are used for comparisons, and a student who doesn't bring home A's and B's can easily feel like a loser. Some young people must feel like the ugly girl who is forced to enter a beauty contest each day of her life. She goes, knowing that not only will she fail but she will never be able to do anything to succeed. If you don't have the muscles or the build, or you lack coordination, in no way can you succeed as an athlete. Being the water boy or the scorekeeper doesn't carry quite the same prestige.

There is a kind of achievement that is available to anyone—and one that is sadly overlooked by many. This kind of achievement does not depend on competing with others, but rather on helping others. It does require skill and knowledge, as well as desire—and is something everyone values. It is proving yourself by becoming outstanding in interpersonal relationships. Read again the opportunities students chose in the *Five Cries* survey. Among those listed were *I want to learn how to make friends and be a friend; I want to be part of a caring accepting group; I want to be part of a group in which there is a frank sharing of personal feelings.* Each of these wants deals with self in relationship with others. Students in this survey placed high value on grades, but they also recognized a universal need—the need to know about oneself, the need to care for and relate to others.

Each of you is a living *potential* resource of caring, which most of you your age crave, especially some who are on their way to feeling like zeros. Even those of you who feel like zeros can be a source of help to others, and if you try, you may find it helps you, too. Also, by learning what to do for others, you will be learning how to improve your own relationships. You'll find you like yourself much more.

There is no time in life when a person is more vulnerable to the treatment of peers than during adolescence. Because this is so, a young person is an important source of happiness or pain to his or her friends and acquaintances. You have the right credentials: your age, similar experiences and problems. You word will be trusted. You are available and need to be useful. Your friends and classmates will turn to you for help, if you will let them. You can help in ways adults can't, no matter how much we care. You can make other young people feel like a "four, or a twenty-six, or even a par seventy-two," as Lucy pointed out to Charlie Brown—but at least something other than a nothing.

William Barclay, a famous theologian, wrote in *Daily Celebration*: "There is nothing more moving in life than to hear someone say, 'I need you; I cannot do without you.' There is no more uplifting feeling than to see someone . . .

facing the tasks of life competently, adequately and gallantly, and to know that you had something to do with equipping him for them" (p. 131).

What Barclay is saying is that someone may turn to you in need. Your help may lead that person to independence, self-respect, worth—to being something other than a zero. I have seen many young people give this kind of help, so I know others can do it too. Many of those who have given this kind of help had to first learn how to do it. You may need to learn this also. The skills of caring are the ones I will be describing and explaining throughout the rest of the book. I know these skills are successful because I have learned and practiced them myself. As young people have learned them and used them, I have seen them face more competently the tasks of their lives. I have seen also the wonderful transformation when they come to like and respect themselves.

IT'S DONE THROUGH PEER COUNSELING

Much of my belief that young people do want to learn how to care about others has come from my work with students in the peer counseling program. Since you're going to be coming across many references to this program in anecdotes and illustrations, I thought you might want to have a brief explanation of what peer counseling is. More details can be found in the last chapter.

The students range in age from eleven to eighteen years. They are trained in small groups taught by two adult leaders. The training follows a carefully developed curriculum, and each session is devoted to a different interpersonal or caring skill. Students talk about what they are learning in the context of their lives and experiences; participate in an activity designed to teach the skill; and examine what they did or didn't learn from doing this. During such "debriefing" of the learning exercise, students share and give feedback to each other, as well as getting instruction and feedback from the leaders. Students are then encouraged to practice the skill before the next session. As the sessions continue, it is hoped that students will begin to experience a group in which frank sharing of feelings occurs; in which they can take off their masks and be the real persons they are; where they can get help in working on their own lack of self-confidence.

When students complete the training, those who want to are given opportunities to help other students who have requested help. These peer counselors are then given supervision and more training if they need it. Much of what peer counselors learn and how they learn it will be included in this book. In this way it may be helpful to readers who want to learn counseling skills on their own.

Since the program began, over three-thousand students in the Palo Alto School District alone have gone through the training. As these students turn to each other and to ones who are forgotten in the back seats of classes and busses and on corners, they are saying, "I need *you* and can I be of help to you, too?" In so doing, some young people are helping to change negative ideas much of society has about youth, using their peer group in positive ways, and discovering how much they are needed by the Cliff Evanses among their acquaintances. You can learn these skills if you want to. If you do, begin with the next chapter.

2

///////////

I Said Hello –
And You Know
What Happened?

"How did you feel when I said to pick a partner?"

"I felt just like I always do when we have to choose up sides in PE," Robert ventured hesitantly.

"I wanted to pick Kathy, but I was afraid she would want to talk to someone else," Lisa blurted out.

"That made me feel good, though," said Kathy softly, "because I don't like to pick people, and I was afraid I wouldn't get chosen."

"Yah, me too. That's why I grabbed Cari, who was sitting next to me," Laura shared.

"Guess I really didn't think anyone would want to talk to me, so I was glad when Greg came over and asked me to be his partner," Steve hesitantly offered as he fidgeted in his chair.

So the feelings of these high school students poured out as they talked about their experiences of trying to have a friendly, comfortable conversation with a member of the class. The assignment was to pick the one whom they knew the least and spend ten minutes getting to know that person better. The purpose was to have students explore what happens when they try to begin a friendship, get in touch with the feelings they have in such situations, and use this as a basis for understanding the basic skills they need to learn to make friends.

In this class, some students couldn't tolerate the ten minutes allowed for this conversation and either walked away to look at magazines or sat and stared in silence. When everyone was asked to come back into the total group to "debrief," most pairs stopped immediately. A few seemed to want to linger. Cari and Laura eventually returned, continuing their conversation as they entered the circle, and sat down together. All the rest walked away from their partners and took their original seats. These observations plus their experiences provided the material for discussing how to talk to strangers: the behaviors that make it more enjoyable and the attitudes one needs in order to do this kindly. These are the skills and feelings one needs if one wants to be a caring person.

As Robert, Lisa, Kathy, and the rest of the class talked, they began describing the thoughts and feelings that hamper them in risking approaching people they don't know in everyday situations. Sometimes it is even hard, they felt, to start a friendly, relaxed conversation with those they *do* know. The fear of possible rejection, of appearing foolish, or of being considered pushy or nosy, are the biggest barriers they feel preventing them from opening friendships with people they do want to know. Not knowing what to say or not feeling witty enough to hold another's attention also came out as fears. Yet some admitted how good it feels when someone comes up to *them* and says, "Hi. I'd like to talk to you." They all seemed amazed and relieved that their feelings and thoughts were also shared by others. Is it, then, a fairly "normal" problem?

If you are among this large group of your peers who suffer from varying degrees of shyness, you also may be relieved to realize you aren't alone in your suffering. Many young people walk down the halls at school seldom speaking to anyone; get lumps in their stomachs thinking about entering a room of young people where they don't know anyone; or want to flee when unexpectedly left alone with guests of their parents whom they have just met. Would it help you to know that quite a number of adults experience these same fears and thoughts when faced with similar social situations? No matter what their education, work, or profession, adults are awkward, appear to be rude, or are as withdrawn as adolescents in many social relationships.

It may be sobering to you to know that people don't necessarily outgrow social fears and awkwardness as they get older. Some don't, perhaps because of what they experienced as adolescents. A counselor working in a community mental health center once shared with me that when he moved to Oregon from Texas as a high school student, he wore his pants rolled up partway, as they did where he came from. The first day no one talked to him. The second day a boy came up to him and said, "Hey, buster, where's the flood?" Forty-year-old Tim, with real emotion in his voice, blurted out, "And boy, did I get those pant legs down fast . . . and I've never forgotten it." Even now, as a successful professional and a husband and father, he is very sensitive about new social situations and particularly careful about the clothes he wears.

Many adults aren't confident in their social life because they never had a chance to learn how to make friends or mingle with others comfortably and confidently. To know how to do this you need a positive attitude toward people and you need to learn what to do in social situations. Both your heart and your head must be involved. This means that you have to work with your heart and your behavior if you really want to make friends and be a friend—if you want to reach out to others in a caring way.

HIDING BEHIND THE MASKS

As I looked around the group assembled for a peer counseling workshop I could hear the heavy silence that enclosed the

room. Thirty pairs of eyes were glued on me, coming from almost expressionless faces. What expressions I saw bordered
on sullenness or apparent boredom. No one fidgeted, smiled,
or even coughed. The temperature rose, seemingly by the
minute. I studied those faces as I took off my jacket, almost
afraid to break the silence by speaking. Here was a mixture of
colors and races. Predominant were the Crow Indian faces
schooled in masking any feelings. Sprinkled here and there
were Chicanos; one black face added further color. This was
a group in which whites were a minority. It was equally divided
between adults and adolescents.

What feelings and fears were hiding behind those masks
worn that afternoon! Soon it was revealed how many were
prisoners of these public postures—and the magnitude of
their struggle to learn how to take the masks off and expose
the sensitive, responsive people beneath who were hungry
for a relationship. Some of the Indians had never seen a
black person before. Many of the Chicanos and whites had
never talked to an Indian before. These were *real* strangers
to one another.

A vision of Florence, an attractive eighth-grade Indian
girl, will always be etched in my memory. After the three
days of training, students were asked to share with the
group what was most meaningful of what they had learned.
Florence sat with eyes wide open between her two shiny,
jet-black braids. After a long silence, she forced words from
her mouth as though she were vomiting. When finished, she
broke into a smile. She didn't have to say what she had
learned. She had demonstrated it—the most basic skill. She
could now say "Hello." And do you know what happened?
The rest of the group clapped!

Florence and Pete and Steve, as well as the adults and the
other students in this high school class, were finally able to
take off their masks and reveal their fears. They were able
to talk about their low self-images and how their mouths
went dry and the physical tensions in them grew as they

attempted to talk to strangers. What helped them to do this was their great desire for help in learning how to find friends and to be friends to members of both sexes. Basically, all of these people wanted to learn how to be caring people—caring friends to themselves and to others. They also knew they needed to learn the first step—how to say hello.

It is sad that our society has caused an isolated peer culture to develop in which you are basically cut off from contacts with adults. But it is tragic that within your own peer culture you isolate yourself from one another, primarily because of your insecurities. The painful realization in this whole process is that you often choose such cruel masks to hide that insecurity. These masks push people farther and farther away from one another and leave scars on sensitive inner selves. There are far too many Cliff Evanses silently walking around, looking and listening for someone even just to smile—if a "Hello" is asking too much.

Stop! Stop and think about the last time you found yourself in an uncomfortable social situation. You know the kind I mean—a time when you felt "on stage." You were asked to say something or demonstrate something in a class; you walked into a class late; you were the last one to arrive at the party; or you were caught alone with someone and were expected to say something. Try to remember exactly what you did at that time. What *did* you say? What did you do? What was the reaction of others? Put your book down and sit for a few minutes and really think. After you have done this, continue reading and see if your behavior fits any of the following "mask" categories. Now—think about those situations.

The Escape Mask

There are a number of ways people "escape" from exposing what they think is their inadequate self. A common one is to escape through professed ignorance or inability rather than to risk making a mistake or not doing it right. Have you ever said "I don't know" to a question, when you really did? Or have you just plain said "I can't do it" when you really could if you tried? It gets people off your back— unless they are persistent.

Another escape is to avoid situations where you might stick out in the crowd, that is, you *think* you would. Students have said that lunch hour is one of these on-stage experiences. They handle it in different ways. Some take books with them to hide behind; others go home at noon if they can; a few try the study hall or talk to a teacher or even get jobs in the cafeteria to fill the void time at lunch. Lunchtime can be painful for many shy young people.

The Aloof or Put-Down Mask

This mask is worn frequently, in various positions and styles. It pushes people away the fastest, although it often hurts the other person when used. We seem to learn quite early and quickly that putting on a mask of boredom or superiority can keep people from finding out how afraid or lonely we really are. The aloof, put-down mask can be effected by a look on the face, a kind of posture, a lift of the eye brow, a sneer or frown, or a tone of voice.

It often is accompanied by attacking words or put-down labels. "Why do we always have to do this dumb stuff?" "This is so boring; why should I be bothered?" are both possible attempts to get out of doing something that might be difficult or exposing. Perhaps when dealing with your own peers you try to shift attention to someone else by calling a person a "jerk," a "nerd," or "stupid"—whatever is the latest put-down label being used.

When working with one group of eighth graders, I observed some of these masks. When asked to pick a companion for a conversation, most spent twenty minutes fooling around to avoid the risk of picking someone. When most were settled in their pairs, several lounged in their chairs with boredom, facing away from their partner. Looking at me with distaste, variations of this question were asked: "What am I supposed to do or say?" The one sitting next to the person asking such a question looked as though he or she wished to become invisible. Some protested, saying, "I don't have anything to say to *her*. Can't I have someone else?" Even knowing that this aloof, bored mask is hiding an insecure person doesn't make the blow any softer.

The Clown or Distractor Mask

If you don't feel you can get positive attention or do something right or well, why not get negative or humorous attention? Or why not divert attention from yourself by doing something that is distracting? You know classmates who crack jokes when it isn't appropriate or who try to turn a serious matter into something humorous without succeeding. There is also the person who picks at someone close by, talks while others have the floor, pulls at notebooks, snatches pens or books. There are people who always giggle or laugh, who seldom ever sit calmly or just smile genuinely. These are all masks for those who haven't learned how to be comfortable with anyone in a one-to-one relationship. These classmates probably realize they annoy others, which increases their insecurity, but they don't know what else to do.

The Clique Mask

Another name for this mask might be "the Bodyguard." This mask is worn by the person who finds a group, whether they like the members or not, to go around with as a shield against social exposure. Most of the time, then, they have someone to be with. They can ignore anyone who is not within the group. It may even shield them against noticing others outside the clique. These classmates may seem confident, poised, and secure. But with their masks off, they frequently have doubts about themselves and think they have to conform in order to belong. Healthy people always will gravitate to people with similar interests, but *not* to the point of excluding those who are different. There is a difference between a group with common interests and the hurtful connotation of "clique." It is true that you will always find within a clique *some* who obviously are concerned about others and who reach out to them. But many young people select this mask to cover up their inability to be an individual and to accept others as individuals.

Which Mask Do You Use?

As you think about your social life—what happens at school, how you treat or get along with classmates—and read about the different masks, can you recognize which ones you use? Or do you have other masks that you put on to cover up your fears or feelings of inadequacy? Would you like to take them off and try a different approach? Even though you haven't hurt another intentionally, would you like to make sure you not only don't hurt someone but might even help another by what you do?

It is an interesting thing about masks. Only the individuals wearing them can choose to take them off. No one can make a law or rule to force you to remove them. It has to be an individual decision based on a desire to be more caring, more genuine, more comfortable with yourself. If you want to, you may want to learn and practice the skills that other young people like Cari, Laura, Lisa, Greg, and Steve have learned. These students experienced a new confidence and satisfaction in their social relations. But even more exciting, they came to believe in their potential for helping the Cliff Evanses they are now noticing around them.

TAKING OFF *YOUR* MASKS

Brenda, a high school junior with long reddish blonde hair and freckles, sat in the group with Florence, the eighth-grade Indian girl. She looked aloof as she sat with quiet composure, neither smiling nor talking, often focusing on me with cold blue eyes. It seemed unfortunate when she later was randomly assigned to work with David, a rather overweight ninth grader, and Dolores, a shy girl her age. The task was to share something about yourself you want to change.

The three sat silently on the floor, looking down, picking at the rug. Joining them on the floor in an attempt to get them started I shared examples of things I want to change about myself. They were reminded that if they were to help others, perhaps experiencing the pain in admitting one's own need for help would be useful. Still there was silence. Then, suddenly, Brenda looked at me and said, "I want to get over being so scared when I'm around kids my age. I want to be more self-confident." All three of us—David, Dolores, and I—silently studied her, realizing Brenda was taking off her mask. You could feel the human warmth going out to her from David, Dolores, and myself. Then David was able to say he wanted to lose weight and improve his body appearance; Dolores shared that she wanted to be more trusting. Brenda's sharing provided courage for the others to take off their masks, too.

A starting point for Brenda in meeting her need was to have her identify someone she admired, someone she would like to model herself after. What was this person like? What did she do that Brenda admired? "Well, she smiles a lot, not stiffly but warmly and relaxed. She seems to enjoy being with people . . . and asks you questions, and is interested in you." Do *you* smile, Brenda? Do you initiate conversations? Do you show others you are interested in them? Or are you concentrating on yourself, trying not to make a mistake, trying to appear cool, smooth, "with it"?

YOU AND THEM ATTITUDE

So the message began with Brenda, and so it begins with you. If you do care about others, if you want to make friends and be a friend, you have to start with your attitude. Shyness originates in self-centeredness. Yes, you have to like yourself, but you can't assume you are so important that everyone is listening intently to everything you say—watching everything you do, evaluating whether you measure up to some vague standard of acceptance. The opposite of self-centeredness is humility—not needing to be right all the time, not having to be better, or even as good as, someone else, knowing you will make mistakes and it's all right.

You have to risk, to initiate, if you want to change the emphasis from you to *them,* if you want to reach out to others. Think about Kathy and Steve who wanted to be picked and thought no one would want them as partners. Remember how pleased they were to have someone initiate a conversation with them. It doesn't matter whether you say it right, or stumble over words or feel shaky inside. They won't notice or care. What matters is that you *approached* someone and probably made him or her feel more like an important person.

As you relax, concentrating on the other, your face will soften. Your mouth can break into a smile. Your eyes will warm up and a glint of pleasure will appear. A message of interest in him or her will be given to your companion.

THE BASIC SKILLS

There are some guidelines you can follow to help you do this. When practiced enough, they become natural skills you will use without thinking. They are suggestions on how to go about starting a conversation with a stranger. This, of course, is a basic skill if you want to reach out to another. You need other skills to develop a relationship, but these will be covered later. It may surprise you to know that young people can grow up, even in cultured, well-educated homes, and not know how to say hello to a stranger. I know quite a number of students who can talk about many subjects, who have large vocabularies, yet find it hard to say that one word—"Hello." Think about the other person who is denied hearing some of the interesting things you could share because you don't know how to start that conversation. The following guidelines have helped some of these uncertain young friends of mine.

• *Introduce yourself first.*

If this is your first meeting, start by giving something— your name. It may not always be appropriate to start this way, but in most situations it does signal the other that you want to have a friendly conversation. If your companion doesn't volunteer his or her name and you want to know it, ask.

• *Use a topic, object, or common surrounding to launch the conversation.*

This can be done with a nonthreatening question, such as, "What bus are you waiting for?" "How's the food this noon?" "What's the score of the game?" These questions obviously would evolve out of something you have in common: a street corner, the school's lunchroom, or a ball game. Or you could talk about a book, a piece of jewelry, or an item of clothing the person is carrying or wearing. "I noticed you have Judy Blume's latest book. I've been wanting to read it. How do you like it? What do you like about it?" The answer you get provides material for the next guideline.

Or as a friend of mine has suggested, you could use the word WHEAT to lead into some topics for starters. Each of the letters is a clue to what you might ask:

W—"Where are you from?"
H—Hobby: "What do you like to do?"
E—Event: something recent or some common experience or knowledge
A—Acquaintance: "Do you know . . . ?"
T—Travel: "Have you been to . . . ?"

By using these methods you probably will get some "free

information"—information that you didn't ask for, that is volunteered, and that can be used to help build the conversation you want to carry on.

- *Use free information to build the conversation.*

Free information that a person adds to the answer of your question often signals what the person really wants to talk about. Nothing people say is insignificant, and when a person adds to, or elaborates on, an answer, this may be the most important information given. For example, if your partner answers your Judy Blume question by merely saying, "I like it a lot," he or she hasn't given you any free information. But if he or she says, "I don't like it as much as *Forever*," you've gotten some information you didn't ask for. You can use this to go further with the conversation. "What did you like so much about *Forever*?" And your conversation should be on its way.

- *Listen.*

Listen not just with your ears, but also with your mind. Don't be preparing your next question while the person is answering your first one. When you do this, you may miss an important piece of free information. You show the other you are listening when you are able to use what the person has just said to ask another question or make a related comment.

- *Avoid "interviewing."*

An interview or an interrogation is asking one question after another without making personal comments yourself or volunteering the same kind of information about yourself that you are asking your companion. A conversation is sharing back and forth. This means you need to give back to the other person some of what you've taken in from what he or she has shared. An example might be "I've read *Forever* too, and what I liked about the book was the honesty in it."

- *Avoid asking questions that can be answered with just a yes or no or a one-word answer.*

When you ask such questions, you lose chances of getting free information. A shy, timid person will say the minimum he or she has to and may just say yes or no. Instead, ask questions that will tend to force your companion to say more than this. For example, the question "How do you like Judy Blume's latest book?" might only cause the person to say: "Not much," or, "It's OK." The question "What do you like about it?" would more likely produce some free information you could use to carry on the conversation.

- *Smile occasionally, but don't laugh or giggle a lot.*

Nervous laughter or giggling is a common mannerism for many people when they are uncomfortable. What usually happens, however, is that it makes the other person uncomfortable too. Smiling too much or laughing with a stranger may cause the other to wonder, "What is so funny about *that*?" or whether he or she is being made fun of. On the other hand, no smiling reduces the friendliness of the conversation.

- *Use a tone of voice that is not phony, but conveys sincerity.*

If you are really sincere, this won't be hard to do. Coming on too strong—that is, talking too loudly, too rapidly, or too long, or giving overdrawn compliments—may turn another away because he or she doubts your sincerity.

- *Allow for silences.*

No one can negotiate a real conversation without some pauses or silences. People need to consider answers, or perhaps a topic has been exhausted and a new direction is needed. We sometimes use silences in conversations as we use periods and paragraphs in writing. A pause may be a period. A silence may be a paragraph, shifting to a new thought.

- *Respect privacy.*

First-time conversations usually don't evolve into intimate sharing. This may come later as a friendship develops. Probing into personal areas the person has not opened up first might be offensive and prevent future contacts with your new friend. Again, listening for free information seems to be the clue. If your companion does not "drop" comments about personal matters, he or she probably is not ready to discuss them.

These are not sophisticated suggestions. They represent common social desires and needs put into action. Use them to test their worth. You need to *prepare* yourself, *practice* them, and *experiment* for this process to become effective and natural.

Preparation

Here's one way to prepare yourself.

- Go to your room where you can be alone and no one can hear you, because you're going to be talking to yourself. You don't want anyone to think you've lost control. I hope there is a mirror, because you will need to use it. Now, study the guidelines to the point where you can remember most of them. Then visualize someone in one of your classes whom you don't know but have noticed: What does this person look like? What is he or she wearing? What objects are in front of him or her? Now, think of an opener you could use to start a conversation. With your mind, see yourself walking up to this person as you are leaving class.

- When you have done this, go to your mirror. Looking at your face, start speaking, saying what you prepared as your opener. It is important to your preparation that you hear your own voice saying those words. You probably won't like the sound, but that doesn't matter. Keep going. Study your face. Are you smiling? Do you show any warmth in your eyes? Perhaps not, at first.

- Think about a possible response your new friend might give you. Then say what you would say to that comment, remembering to feed back some information about yourself. Imagine what he or she might say next. How could you build the conversation from here?

- Do all of this several times more, attempting to smile and warm up. At first, you may feel clammy imagining yourself doing this, but with practice, it gets more natural and less frightening.

Before actually putting your preparation into action, think about the worst thing that could happen to you as a result. Ask yourself what you will do if the person turns away or gives you a weird look or puts you down—all the things you fear might happen in a social situation. Now say to yourself, "But this is only an experiment. I have nothing to lose. I'm practicing, and it didn't kill me. I'm still alive." Realizing you can survive the worst thing you can imagine can give you courage to go out and try.

Practicing

After peer counselors have reviewed the guidelines and practiced them in class with other students, they practice outside the class. They are asked to approach a stranger to evaluate the results when used away from the class setting. Their experiences make them believers! "I said hello . . . and you know what happened?" One high school girl went right from the session to a college cafeteria for lunch, sat down next to an adult, and opened the conversation. "You know, after a couple of questions he began talking about his interest in Eastern religions, and I never had to say another thing! And he thanked me for talking to him when I got up to leave."

You can practice, too. It would probably help if you could get a couple of your friends to try it also, so you could share your experiences. But it can be done alone. You could consider it an experiment. Make a contract with yourself that by a certain time, such as the end of the week, you will have tried to start two conversations with people you don't know.

Experimenting

When you decide you are ready, why not make your first trial run with adults? Adults are more experienced in carrying on casual conversations. You might experiment first with a gas station attendant. They usually like to talk. Or maybe start with an adult standing next to you in a ticket line, or a seat partner on a bus. Pick a situation where your time is limited so you won't be too taxed in using your new skills. After a few practice sessions with adults, contract with yourself to approach a classmate.

Keep a diary or journal to record what you did and what happened. As part of your entries, review what you didn't do and wished you had. Then decide what you will work on the next time you try this. Make another contract with yourself. Write down any feelings of satisfaction you feel or any new sign of increased confidence on your part. Begin reviewing your whole week to remember times you initiated a conversation spontaneously, on the spur of the moment. This is evidence that the skills are becoming yours. They are becoming part of your personality and natural behavior.

SINCERELY YOU

Having a conversation with someone may seem insignificant to you—especially if you have never had to work at being able to do this. Since so many of you have said so, I've assumed this is a topic that is important to you. But have you stopped to think about what a precious gift your conversation may be to someone else? This is especially true when it is a warm, sincere conversation. To a Cliff Evans or to many of your own classmates, being approached and having a peer show genuine interest in them can be the greatest thing that happened that day. Even a warm, cheerful "Hello" from an unexpected person can add a glow to the day.

But the act, the reaching out, must be sincere, or it will fail and even be hurtful to the other. It is sincerity that erases awkwardness and makes inaudible the stumbling words you may get out. Here's an example of what can happen when you aren't sincere:

When Ed was a new student in his school, the student body president was assigned to be his pal for the day. This boy seemed warm and was outgoing, making Ed really feel good. The next day, however, when Ed met the president in the hall and eagerly approached him to talk, the president greeted him with a stare and brushed him aside. "It would have been far better to be left alone on the first day than to be led to believe he really was interested in me," Ed said, as he gulped back the tears.

Anyone can learn techniques and use them mechanically. They can even use them as weapons. Techniques or human relations skills without heart become sterile and are like phony manipulations. Genuine caring for another requires learning some skills and then using them while listening to what your heart tells you. Perhaps, you know, the more you try to express sincere care for another, the more you will come actually to care for others—and for yourself, too.

What happens to you socially during these critical formative years can strengthen your self-image or leave emotional scars that you may carry all your life. If someone reaches out to you, or you reach out to someone, self-esteem is built and another brick is put on the foundation of a healthy adult person. But if you blurt out, "Hey buster, where's the flood?" or make fun of an awkward peer or ignore the girl who sits alone day after day at lunch, you are contributing to forming scars, and you yourself may be losing out, too. If anything can be done to prevent such wounds, we will all live in a kinder world. This could begin to happen if you'll only start with "Hello," and see what happens.

REACHING OUT THROUGH PEER COUNSELING

In my experience the idea for a peer counseling program came from listening to students talk about two things: their lack of personal confidence in relationships with their peers and their desire to help others. It started before the data were gathered for the *Five Cries of Youth* book that I mentioned earlier. You may remember these data showed how many students want to be part of a caring, accepting group. The students in this study also wanted to learn how to deal with their lack of self-confidence and how to make friends and be a friend.

Students in this program voluntarily give up their own time to take the eighteen-hour training program that prepares them to become peer counselors. What they learn also helps them to cope with their own lives and with the expectations of society as they are moving into adulthood. The training method provides students with a group in which they can learn and practice human caring skills in a safe environment.

The first skill that peer counselors must learn is how to approach someone they don't know and begin a comfortable, friendly conversation. If they can't do this, it will be difficult for them to reach out to help or counsel a peer. As I mentioned earlier, students are asked to practice before their next session. Their preparation for doing this is talking to another member of the group for ten minutes and discussing what happened. This has proved to be a fairly safe way of initiating the training process. Because they can experience the immediate relevance of this first session, most students in training begin to take off their masks, trusting the other students to help them learn the skills being taught.

You don't have to have such a group, but it helps. It particularly helps if you have an adult as a leader who is observant and sensitive to what you are doing and to your feelings. It is helpful also because the total emphasis is on learning how to care and reach out to others. These training groups are not group counseling; they are educational classes, using a process that points a person away from self—toward others.

Many students come to peer counseling training feeling they have nothing to give to anyone else. They are shy, feel unattractive, are even labeled as behavior problems. They want help for themselves. Because training is open to anyone without having to "qualify," they can get this help with a sense of dignity, rather than one of admitted failure. As they learn they realize others have similar problems. They are needed. They *do* have something to give. Each one of you does, and your giving begins with "Hello"—then see what happens!

3

//////////

What Do You Ask?

The other night I watched the Johnny Carson show. I laughed at how interested I became, listening to his guests talk, answering questions I would have liked to ask if I had had the chance. What a low-keyed talent Carson has to gently bring out the interesting things about the guest he is interviewing and make it fascinating to the listening audience! While he does this, even the guest seems to enjoy what is happening. As I watched, I realized that he was demonstrating the effective art of asking questions and listening— asking the questions people in the audience, as well as his guest, wanted asked, and listening carefully to create new questions from the answers. He was doing all this under the pressure of lights, cameras, and a huge audience. That has to be an art!

It may be quite a jolt to you to go from reading about trying nervously to start a conversation with a stranger to thinking about interviewing celebrities on TV. But there is a connection. Johnny Carson did not come "ready-made" with such skills. He had to learn them. If you had known him when he was young, he may have been as shy and uncomfortable in conversations as you are now. You may not be able to become a Johnny Carson, nor might you want to be. But you *can* learn the basic skills he uses. If you do, or even try, you may find life more exciting.

The skills he demonstrates are really twofold: the ability

to ask questions so a person can share himself or herself with another, and the ability to listen to words, feelings, and behaviors. These are the skills you want if you want to make friends and be a friend to others. It helps to learn them if you also care about both yourself and others. When these skills are learned and used consistently, human relationships and friendships are improved. So are marriages and families.

Because both skills, that is, questioning and listening, are equally important, I'm going to talk about them separately. In this chapter, I'll concentrate on questioning. The next chapter will take up "What Do You Hear?" which of course means "How do you listen?" But first let's see how good you can get at letting people tell you what they want to say.

THE QUESTIONS WE DO—AND COULD—ASK

Annette screwed up her face with concern as she began talking. "Last Sunday I was talking to a new friend at church. We both enjoy horses and often ride together. As we talked, she casually mentioned she had helped arrange the flowers on the altar that morning in memory of her father. Even though I knew she had given me some 'free' information, I wasn't prepared. I didn't know what to say. All I could think of was 'Ask an open-ended question!' but I couldn't think of one . . . so I didn't say anything. I've felt bad about this all week."

"What kinds of open-ended questions could Annette have asked?" I asked the students around me.

"When did your father die?" Liz volunteered.

"No, that's a closed question because she could just say, 'last year,' or whatever," snapped John.

"How about, 'What were you feeling while you fixed the flowers?'" Dori offered.

"Or, 'What other things have you done in his memory?'"

"Maybe, 'How have you and your family adjusted to losing your father?'" Shawna suggested.

"Yes," said David, "or, 'What has been the most difficult thing for you since your father died?'"

"I can think of some myself—now. But I was so shocked when she said that, I couldn't think of anything," moaned Annette, still distressed.

Annette and the others listened as I reminded them that when we are upset, nervous, or self-conscious, our minds don't work well. A kind of static seems to appear that gets in the way, and our thoughts become confused and uncertain. This is why repeated practice of asking open-ended questions when you aren't nervous helps you be able to do it when you are nervous.

As the discussion continued, the group finally became silent. The message was sinking in. If you want to be a caring person, knowing how to ask personal, caring questions is an important skill to learn. Annette broke the silence, timidly asking, "Do you think it is too late to ask her a question about this, next Sunday?"

The "What" Versus the "How" Questions

It's no fun when your mind goes blank, and you lose your speech, and your mouth feels so dry it seems as though glue has stuck your lips together—and you're supposed to be carrying on a conversation. Everyone has had this happen to them, including Johnny Carson. They have, because nature has a way of preparing one for a physical reaction to threat, whether it is a physical or an emotional fear. The sympathetic (the emergency) division of the nervous system takes over and a lot of things happen—the heart beats faster; you breathe more rapidly; the digestion process comes almost to a halt (eat very lightly when you are very angry or nervous); perspiration may break out on the palms of your hands or on your forehead; and almost always the salivary glands stop functioning—your mouth goes dry. Nature is alerting you to do something. Either run away or fight! So, you see, what happens to you is *natural* to all human beings.

Maybe this happened to you when you experimented

with what I suggested in the last chapter. You were able to open the conversation but never heard a word the other person said—because your mind went blank. You didn't know what to say next. You probably couldn't even see, let alone hear.

Maybe it wasn't that bad. But perhaps after you started you didn't know where to go with the conversation. The guy you approached said the book he was carrying was his computer science book and he was on his way to the computer center to test his new FORTRAN program. You didn't know a computer spoke a language and you wouldn't have recognized a FORTRAN if you met it, or him, on the street. So you didn't know what to say next. You decided this conversation business was not for you—that the next time you tried it, it would be with someone you knew who spoke *your* language.

What went wrong? Are you sure you only want to talk with friends who have the same interests and experiences you have? If so, won't you be pretty limited? You'll miss meeting people along the way who could add to your life or who could use your help.

Here are some examples of what could happen. Go through them and see if any fit what happened to you when you opened your conversation:

1. You asked only questions that could be answered yes or no. You didn't throw out enough conversational rope for your companion to take hold of to draw you both into closer contact, or to expand the conversation further.
2. You ignored free information that was subtly or quietly tucked into the other's answers.
3. Your nervousness caused you to do most of the talking or to ask one question after another.
4. You failed to explore enough topics to find one you both really wanted to talk about.
5. You weren't sufficiently *interested* in the other to lead that person to talk about him- or herself comfortably.
6. You didn't realize that the other person was concentrating

on something else, or didn't feel good, or didn't want to talk.

All of these, including the last one, are common mistakes we make when we are awkward in making conversation. Sometimes people don't want to talk. Perhaps they will later, but not now. It's got nothing to do with you. People try to tell us in different ways, but we miss the clues and keep pushing until the conversation dies with a thud. If this happens to you, don't get discouraged. When you recognize these clues and when you know how and when to use different kinds of questions, your mistakes will be fewer. As this happens you will discover how much fun it can be to talk to different people.

CONVERSATIONAL TOOLS

Questions are tools we use to gather different kinds of information. These tools, or questions, come in four different shapes. Each one can be used to help you discover different ways of knowing people. These four kinds are

1. the closed-ended question, which gathers one-word or one-sentence answers
2. the informational question, which searches for specific information or facts
3. the open-ended question, which collects varied kinds of information
4. the personal question, looking for the other's feelings, opinions, and attitudes.

Some of the tools can be combined. For example, you can ask an open-ended informational question or a closed informational one. The point is, know your tools—how to use them and when to use them effectively in conversations. When you interchange the kinds of questions you use, you can pace a conversation, shift the mood, or expand the topic. By using a variety and combination of questioning, you can develop closer relationships.

All of you seem to know how to use closed-ended and

informational questions, because you use them most of the time. You might also know how to ask about feelings, but you don't seem as confident in doing it. The open-ended question seems the hardest to use naturally, and that's too bad because it's the most useful tool in your conversational tool kit.

Let's see what you *do* know about these tools called questions: Imagine you are with a group of young people. You are asked to share two of your most unusual interests—hobbies, activities, or things you do that turn you on. Many love to play tennis, ski, or swim, but do you have some different interests that most people don't know that you have? Think about this a minute, but if you draw a blank, don't let it bother you. Not all of us have "creative" or unusual interests.

As I have asked many to do this, I have heard about some fascinating interests: camping, explosives, collecting antique rock candy molds, rock polishing, Egyptology, Bible reading, bottles, planning children's playgrounds, cake decorating, sitting on the beach, phenomenology, hunting, and on and on. Could you add to my "collection" of unusual pastimes?

Now let's do a question test. Pick the interest from the ones above about which you know the least. Phenomenology probably tops the list, but that might be a stopper. What is it, anyway? Maybe "planning children's playgrounds" would be easier. How much do you know about this subject, other than having seen or used a playground?

Write down all the questions you could ask a person who has this interest. Suppose someone said, "I'm fascinated with planning children's playgrounds." Besides the comment, "Oh?" how could you take that information and build a conversation? Since you may often complain you don't know what to say in conversations, here is a chance to test out what you can do when not actually engaged in conversation under pressure. Before you read the ideas below, see what you can do on your own. If you really try, you will be practicing your questioning skills.

Possible Questions to Ask About Planning Children's Playgrounds

1. How long have you been interested in this?
2. Do you have any training for it?
3. Why are you interested?
4. What kinds of materials or equipment do you like to use?
5. What turns you on about this activity?
6. How did you get started?
7. Where do you do this?
8. Do you build them yourself?
9. Do you get paid for it?
10. Have you ever had any of your plans used?
11. How do you feel when you see children playing on one you designed?
12. Do you plan to make this into a career?
13. What talents or skills do you need to do this?
14. Are there others who do this, too? Is it a kind of profession?
15. Where do you get your ideas?
16. How long does it take you to do it?
17. Are there certain things you put into every one you design?
18. How do you sell your ideas?
19. Do you think you'll ever lose interest in this?
20. What is your greatest achievement, the one that makes you the most proud?

These questions were asked of Wendy, a young graduate student attending a leadership training seminar. Would you have thought of some of them?

Before checking your own list of questions—you *do* have a list, don't you?—go through this one and identify the kind of question you think each one is, that is, *closed, open-ended, informational,* or *personal,* or any combination of these categories. For example, a question might be open-personal

(O-P). If you have trouble, review the definitions discussed a few pages back. As I interpret these questions, I found

10 Closed
 3 Informational
 4 Open-Personal
 3 Open-Informational

A key to the "right" answers is located at the end of the chapter. Before checking your score against it, go over the list again to see how many you have in each category. Then consult the key. Now check your own list of questions. How many of yours were open-ended, closed, informational, or personal?

If you are like most people thinking of questions, you probably found on your list more closed questions than open; more informational than personal. If you are following this pattern in your actual conversations, you are limiting the information another can give you, and you are probably also limiting the material you get to build bridges between you and the other person.

Even more important is the fact that closed, as well as informational, questions choke the sharing of shy, withdrawn people—the very ones you want to reach. These questions choke because they don't ask enough. Shy people are afraid to share. They have to be given "permission" to open up. Also, shy people often fear they can't give the right answer. The poised conversationalist can take a closed or informational question and add to it, adding more information than asked. But unskilled conversationalists are afraid to do this or don't know how. This means you've got to know how to ask the questions that help them give information, when to do this, and how to ask them comfortably. This is the art of a genuinely kind person.

The skill of asking open-ended questions is not very hard to learn. Merely by changing one or two words, a closed question can be converted to an open one. Using our list of questions, I'll show you how it's done.

CLOSED	OPEN
2. Do you have any train- ing for this?	What kind of training have you had for this?
8. Do you build them yourself?	What things do you do to help in the building of these playgrounds?
10. Have you ever had any of your plans used?	How have your plans been used?

Notice how the open questions help Wendy to tell you much more about herself and give you free information you can use to build the conversation further.

After you try using open-personal questions you will discover an important fact about human behavior: People of any age *prefer* being asked the questions that allow them to tell you about themselves! This kind of question permits them to say as much or as little as they care to, including how they feel about things. Knowing this, isn't it sad that most of us are programmed to ask closed questions?

I've learned this through the peer counseling training lesson on questioning. After questions have been suggested, as in our example of Wendy, the person who is being asked about an interest is asked to choose three questions from the list he or she would most *enjoy* answering. Usually the person picks open-personal questions or open-informational ones. Wendy chose: "What turns you on about this activity?" "What kinds of materials or equipment do you like to use?" and "What is your greatest achievement?" Her answers revealed interesting things about her personality, her knowledge, and her accomplishments—and *she* could decide what she wanted to emphasize with details or feelings. People *appreciate* a chance to share what they know, can do, and have accomplished. Why not? We talk enough about our faults, why not our strengths?

A friend told me what happened when she tried to practice this skill with her son. Every day when he came home from school she asked him how school was that day. He would mumble something as he put his books down on the way to his room. Then one day when he came home, she stopped what she was doing and in a quiet, sincere voice asked, "Ken, how did you feel about school today?" Ken stopped, put down his books, drew up a chair, and began talking. When he finished, she asked what was different about what she asked that made him so willing to share. He thought a minute and said, "Well, you always ask me how school was today . . . so there's nothing to say. The buildings are still standing, the trees are still there. But when you ask me how I *feel* about school today—that's different. That's today and what happened to *me*."

What kinds of questions are *you* asking during a typical week? It might be interesting to keep a record of them and study what they say about your conversational questioning. Are many of them repetitious or monotonous? What kinds of questions would *you* like to be asked, and by whom? Maybe most of your friends don't ask you anything about yourself. You wish they would. You might feel they were more interested in you. Then you'd feel more like a true friend.

What kind of questions do *you* ask? When was the last time you asked your mom or dad how she or he was feeling, and really meant it? Have you asked Mary what scares or excites her about graduating in June? Or did you ask Mike what it felt like to score the winning point in the soccer game? Don't screw up your face in horror, thinking, Kids don't ask questions like *that!* No, many of them don't, and that's the problem. What *you* want asked, others do, too. Why don't you be the one to start? See how much more caring goes into your friendships as a result.

QUESTIONS THAT HURT

Open-ended questions work, even when you could care less about the answer—or the person asked. "I asked him about Eastern religions, and I thought he would never stop. Boy, was I bored!" The girl who said this is unkind. Besides, she is phony. She was asking for information she didn't want. This is the noncaring side of human relations skills. Questions can be used to help or to hurt. Manipulating a person to expose feelings and interests leaves him or her vulnerable. When we react with boredom or put-downs we injure the security of the other. The caring person wants to prevent hurt, not cause it.

Thoughtless use of questioning skills can hurt *you* too. Eventually, kids will avoid you or shove you away. Everyone with a pittance of sense stays away from situations where they have been hurt—and self-exposure has a very sensitive skin that burns easily. The other person's safety valve for protection is sensing whether you are sincere. Just saying the right words is not convincing. You have to really want to hear the answer, or you become the phony. The same words carry different meanings depending on a tone of voice, an emphasis, an attentiveness coming from the face and eyes. "How do you feel about . . . ?" can be asked with no interest while your eyes roam. But, "How do *you* feel about . . . ?" stimulates an honest answer when asked gently while pausing and expectantly waiting for the answer.

I don't think any of you want to be phony. You hate it. So you are puzzled sometimes, wondering what you should do when you know more about a subject than the person you are getting to know. You may know a lot about the subject, but here the subject is not the critical issue. You aren't doing research. You are, you hope, trying to get to know a *person* better. Forget what you know. Find out what your *friend* thinks, feels, or knows about the topic. As he or she talks about ideas, pleasures, opinions, filtered through his or her own experience and personality, you'll come away knowing a human being in more depth. You might even learn something about the subject at the same time. But if not, you will still have added to the other person's self-worth, and that's a precious gift. If we really want to know a person, no matter how expert we are on a topic, we'll still find things to ask, because we want to hear and understand how the other reacts to the topic.

Often we are tempted to correct misinformation we hear. If it is important to do this, because, for example, the other person's welfare is endangered by his or her inadequate knowledge, do so gently. Let the other "save face." You might say something like, "I've heard it differently," or, "There's some evidence on the other side." Avoid saying, "You're wrong," or a flat, cold, "I disagree with you." Remember, you are concerned about the *person*, not the information.

What do you ask? Are your questions used like a sword—or like an extended hand? By pushing yourself aside to let your companion get the attention, you will have not only the skill, but the kindness, to coach your friend to share the richness and uniqueness of him- or herself. To do this is to put honesty into the words, "I care."

SCORING KEY FOR IDENTIFYING QUESTIONS

Code: C=Closed Questions
I=Informational Questions
O=Open-ended Questions
P=Personal Questions
C-I=Closed-Informational
O-P=Open-Personal
O-I=Open-Informational

Question	1. C	6. O-I	11. O-P	16. C
	2. C	7. I	12. C	17. C
	3. O-P	8. C	13. I	18. O-I
	4. O-I	9. C	14. C	19. C
	5. O-P	10. C	15. I	20. O-P

4

//////////

What Do You Hear?

Have you ever played on a seesaw? When I was a child, every time we went to a park, that's where I headed first. The greatest fun was trying to hold my side down, with my partner stuck in the air. If I was heavy enough, or could dig my heels in, I was successful. But I often got caught when my playmate quickly slid down on top of me and then jumped off. At times I was able to bounce my friend off at the top. Occasionally he or she would get a skinned knee or a bumped chin. Then the fun ended with tears.

Conversations are like seesaws. Motion is created back and forth by asking questions and listening to answers. Questions start the seesaw; listening keeps it going.

You can "bump off" a person in a conversation by asking phony questions or by interrogating with a series of closed-ended questions. You can leave a person stranded in the air, or immobile on the ground, by not listening or by doing all the talking and not inviting any comments or responses from the other. This kind of treatment can hurt. Your companion may not walk off crying, but he or she may not want to talk to you again. Remember the time that I described in Chapter 3 when Annette was talking to her friend after church? Well, this was an example of how Annette bumped off her friend by not asking anything about her father's death. Maybe the friend felt slightly bruised, and alone, because she felt Annette had not heard what she was wanting to tell her. Even if Annette's response had been stumbling, perhaps the seesaw of the conversation could have been kept going. It might have developed to where the friend could have talked about the hurts or sadness connected with losing her father.

Are *you* a good listener? If so, why do you think you are—or aren't? What *is* a good listener? Students who feel they are say it is because they pay attention; remember what the person says; and ask questions based on what the other has said; or it is because they like people and are interested in them. They feel they are poor listeners when they think about something else while the other is talking or when they're tired, irritated, or depressed. Such answers partly define "how we hear." They also point to what each student thinks "good" means, and how much they actually know about real listening.

In fact, there are a variety of ways to listen, just as there are a variety of ways to say something. Human beings are complex and concealing. Often we don't say what we want to say, or say exactly the opposite of what we want to say. Sometimes, we aren't honest or direct with another because we think we don't have the right or are afraid of what will happen if we are. The body "talks," too, sometimes more honestly than the tongue. Have you ever realized how much you say by your facial expressions? People also express themselves eloquently in their music, art, or dance.

These different ways of talking need different ways of listening. To keep the seesaw going in conversations and in relationships, we need to understand and use these different ways, especially if our goal is to be a caring, thoughtful person. By knowing how to listen in various ways, you can be accurate in picking up messages no matter how they are masked or distorted or how they are delivered. Some messages are heard just by listening silently; some, by holding a hand or giving a hug. But to be able to respond accurately, you need to *hear* accurately.

Most people listen only with their ears. Too few listen with their hearts as well as their ears, listening to the other's sharing of his or her hopes, joys, fears. Only listening with our ears may happen when we are emotionally tired or are struggling with personal problems. Sometimes we just don't want to hear. Erma Bombeck had this happen to her, and what she experienced might help you to avoid this. She confessed that when she "woke up" she never detested herself more than at that moment.

Erma had had a hard week, and up until the time she was to go to the airport the day had been one in which she had been besieged by what she called assaults on her ears. She was ready to be alone, to relax and read, while she waited to board the plane. As she settled into her book, she heard a voice next to her, belonging to an elderly woman, saying, "I'll bet it's cold in Chicago." Without smiling, Erma returned flat, clipped responses to what the woman said. Nevertheless, the woman continued talking, soon unfolding that she was taking her husband's body to Chicago to be buried. After fifty-three years of marriage, he had suddenly died. With a start, Erma's heart woke up. She realized another human being was screaming to be heard and in desperation had turned to *any* stranger. This woman wasn't asking for advice, information, or even consolation. She wanted a living person just to be willing to be "present" while she talked. The woman talked numbly and steadily until it was time to board the plane. Then she moved on to find her seat in another section. As Erma hung up her coat, she heard the woman's plaintive voice say to her new seat companion, "I'll bet it's cold in Chicago." Erma prayed, "Please, God, let her listen."

Yes, Erma, Please, God, let *me* listen—to my loved ones when they irritate me or interrupt me; to my colleagues when they dominate meetings by talking too much or criticizing me and others; to my young friends when their fragile, delicate self-images cause them to be cruel or unkind in what they do and say. Let me listen to what is really being said. Provide me with the desire to care and the knowledge of what I need to learn or do so that I *can* listen.

Heart listening can be learned, but it cannot be practiced or done mechanically. You can listen mechanically with your ears, but not with your heart. Why? Because the essence of listening with your heart is to put your whole self into trying to hear what the other is saying, because you care that much. Unless you care, you won't stop talking, resisting, or ignoring long enough to hear what is being said. You won't sacrifice your time or convenience to hear the other's feelings behind the words or the twisted behaviors. If you care enough, you will learn the necessary skills, and then you will practice repeatedly, putting out the effort needed to learn to listen with your heart.

TEACH *ME* TO LISTEN

Wanting to learn is the first step. The *desire* is basic. Desire comes from the heart. When it's true, you become more alert. You forget yourself. You try harder to hear. Add to desire some of the guidelines I teach to peer counselors, practicing them and reviewing them, and you'll find gradually that your listening has changed, become more sensitive, more accurate—more caring.

Your Listening Filter

A filter is a device that strains out something, allowing some, but not all, of what is being filtered to pass through. The type of material used in a filter depends on what you want or don't want to pass through it. The quality and texture determines how much or how little will get through. Sometimes a filter becomes clogged, preventing anything at all from flowing through.

There are filters inside our head and "heart" that sort, strain, hold back, or let pass information we hear or see. Human filters are made of experiences, knowledge, biases,

values, emotions. All of these materials combine to determine the fineness or coarseness of the mesh and, thus, how
much we let through to our minds and feelings. Sometimes
these filters become clogged by fear, anxiety, depression, or
sadness, preventing us from hearing anything. Until these
emotions pass, our listening is impaired.

Guideline #1

Become familiar with your listening and observing filter.
Notice the biases and values that may influence what you
remember or the interpretation of what you hear.

No one has or wants a neutral listening filter system. How
dull we would be if we did! The important thing is to be
familiar with how our individual filters *are* biased. A typical
bias is the one that only hears and remembers negative facts
or opinions. Another is one that lets only the positive messages go through. Some have a bias that turns compliments
into criticisms or put-downs, believing nothing good said
about them could be true. Is it true that "popular" students
only say interesting things, whereas quiet or shy classmates
are always "dull"? If this seems to be true, could there be a
listening filter that is functioning with a bias? Think about
your own particular listening filter. When you do, maybe
you'd like to change it, or adjust it, especially if you are
really trying to be a caring person even when you listen.

Peer counselors are asked to examine their biases or filters
in order to become better listeners. To help them improve
their listening, they participate in an activity similar to the
"Gossip" game. Four students are selected to be the listeners. Three leave the room while one stays. The rest of the
group are asked to listen until the game is over. The one
who stays is read a description of Paul, a true story about a
former student. When the reading of the story about Paul is
finished, the listening student goes out and selects one of the
three outside the room to bring in. Then, in front of the

group, the first listener tells the second listener what he or she heard from the reading, and the group listens to the second telling of Paul's story. This procedure continues until all the students outside have been brought in, the second listener telling the third and so on. Here is a brief summary of what is read:

PAUL

Paul's teachers are glad that he has finally graduated from the ninth grade and will be going to high school. They are relieved that he will no longer be in their classes. Although he is good-looking and charming, he has given every teacher a hard time.

Paul's main interests are girls and sports. Since he has a nice build, lots of blonde hair, clear blue eyes, and a smooth, gracious, shy manner, it is easy for him to pursue both interests. He has above-average ability, but seldom seems to use it. He gets into trouble by talking and clowning in class, coming late, or skipping school. He turns in his work late and has had many visits with the dean. His mother is called to school often because of Paul's problems. She seems cooperative but doesn't know what to do.

All Paul's friends have similar problems. They are known as the tough guys, as burnouts, and as troublemakers. Associating with this group, Paul has gotten into fights and trouble with the police, and had one arrest in the eighth grade.

Paul's father didn't go to college, but he is a successful regional manager for a drug company. This means that he travels a lot, is seldom home, and leaves his wife to handle the problems of the family.

During his ninth-grade year, Paul was active in student government and went out for football. He's good in sports, but didn't take football seriously. He made the coach mad by his casual attitude and late appearances at practice. But though he had poor grades in the seventh and eighth grades, he did improve in the ninth, earning a D only in math. It is obvious that Paul likes people and wants to be liked by them. Yet he still seems lost and confused, choosing to depend on his personality and to devote his time to socializing.

What did *you* hear from reading about Paul? Do you like him? What are your impressions of Paul? What points would you pick out if you were asked to tell the story of Paul to someone else? Write these down without rereading the description of Paul—then look at what you've written. What evidence does this give of *your* listening filter? What *did* stick in your mind? This is a real test, because you had the advantage of being able to *read* it. Others only get to *hear* it read. Now, please take a minute and write out your impressions or things you remember before reading further.

Many young people don't like Paul. A girl once *did* start her retelling of the story by saying, 'I'm going to tell you about a boy you're really going to like." Immediately her "listener" pricked up his ears to listen for good things. But most students, in relating what they heard about Paul, emphasize his negatives—poor grades, the arrest, the crowd he went around with, and the trouble he made for teachers. Many students blame his parents. Most forget—or don't hear—that his grades improved, that he has a pleasant personality, and that he has above-average ability.

How would you explain this? Could it be because of their listening filters? We may not be proud of realizing what our filters are doing to our listening, but when it's brought to our attention, we can do something to change our filters. One girl almost cried when she told her classmates that she felt she was listening to a description of herself when she was Paul's age. Certain associations triggered a memory chain. When this happened, she "heard" only that which seemed to describe herself at that age.

Many see themselves in Paul. Some don't like to admit it because they know people don't like tough guys or kids who get arrested. If a listener doesn't like the image he or she gets of Paul, the filter blots out his positive traits and qualities, such as his improvement in the ninth grade.

What could you learn about listening from all of this? Does this tune you in to the way you listen to others, such as your parents, brothers, sisters, teachers, or friends? Does the way you listen interfere with being able to make friends? Is it possible that this awareness might help you adjust your filter so that you might listen more accurately and perhaps more positively to people—even some you think you don't like?

Does That Word Mean . . . ?

Conversation seesaws are fascinating, because we dress our messages with different words, accents, and tones of voice, just as we dress our bodies with colors, styles, and accessories. Combined words and sentences create thoughts and impressions just as clothes and behavior create an image. However, it's must easier to see shades of color and the fit of clothes than it is to understand the meaning of words and sentences. This may be because we are often more sloppy in dressing our thoughts than we are in dressing our bodies. Young people are so casual and "sloppy" with their words that they seem at times to have a language of their own.

I have just given you a perfect example of what I mean. I used the word *sloppy*. *Sloppy* has different meanings—if you don't know how *I* am using it, you don't really know what I am trying to say. If you were to ask, I'd say that *sloppy* means to use vague, repetitious terms or words to express broad kinds of feelings or meanings that can be interpreted any way you want to. To me "sloppy" words are words like *good, bad, far out, for sure, awesome, right on, jam, moving out*—or even *love* or *care*. If a listener doesn't push for a more precise, clear meaning of how the speaker is using these coined or overworked words, then his or her interpretation of the message may be inaccurate. When I am vague, *you* have to fill in the meaning, and that meaning may be different from the one I really wanted to express. Here's an example from a training session:

During the listening activity, Wanda told Pete that Paul often "hassled" his teachers. *Hassled* was the word Wanda used to describe what Paul was doing to his teachers—giving them a hard time. Pete, however, told *his* listener that Paul often "hustled" his teachers, a word commonly used to describe pressuring for sexual relationships. Actually, Pete was trying to say that Paul gave his teachers a bad time by irritating them. Becky knew the meaning of the word *hustle* so she passed on to *her* listener that Paul was trying to "make out" with his teachers. So a totally different message was passed on as a result of the use of a "sloppy" word. This would not have happened if Pete had merely said that Paul irritated his teachers by interrupting them and disturbing others.

Guideline #2

Ask the meaning of words you don't understand or ask how a word is being used in the context of the message before proceeding with, or ending, a conversation. Establish the habit of asking, "What do you mean by . . . ?" "Could you give me an example of how you are using the word . . . ?" If asked sincerely, you will be showing you are listening and are also wanting to understand accurately.

Listen for Feelings Not Expressed by Words

When describing a good listener we often use the expressions "She was really 'with' me when I talked," or "He understood." What this means is that the listener understood more than the literal meaning of the words used. He or she understood the feelings being expressed, so the person talking felt the listener's *total* presence during the conversation. The listener's heart, as well as head, was listening. The head can unscramble the meaning of words, but the heart has to be listening to understand the feelings beneath those words. I'm sure you have friends who listen to your words and have occasionally had friends who also listen to your feelings, so you know the difference. You may not have been able to explain exactly what the difference was—but you *experienced* the difference. The important thing, though, is whether *you* can listen with your heart to the feelings of others.

Suppose Paul came to you to tell you about himself. Imagine how he would look as he talked to you. Hear the possible tone of voice he might use. What feelings could you "hear" by studying his face? As he talked of clowning, coming late to class, not turning in his work, giving his mother trouble, and running around with the crowd he runs with, how does his voice shift and what are his eyes and hands doing? Just looking at his total body, what feelings do you hear? Would you hear "I want to be important. I want to be noticed"? Would you hear, "I don't feel good about myself. I'm afraid of failing; I'm not liked or respected by the 'good' guys at school?"

No, Paul wouldn't come right out and say things like that. He may not be sure even that this is how he feels. But if you let him know, gently, without judging, that this is what you thought you heard, what might happen? He might deny it. Or, he might begin to open up and be more direct about his feelings, concerns, and possible fears. If you continued to listen with your heart, he might find he really could trust you.

Listening for underlying meanings or feelings is hard to do. It can be risky. It takes great concentration to sort out feelings from the words you hear or the actions you see. But I found it is very important to do this. Whenever I was depressed or had a problem and was expressing it the best I could to a dear friend, he often got angry, criticizing me rather than trying to understand. I knew he cared about me, but I was hurt by how he reacted to what I was trying to say. Then I began to listen myself, with my heart, and I heard what *he* was trying to say. His anger was his way of saying, "I care, but I don't know how to help."

You and I need to be heard. Our friends do, too. To hear clearly we need to venture beyond words to open the secret doors of the moods and feelings suggested by the words. It's safer to stay outside, dealing only with the usual meaning of the words. It takes courage to go inside, to discover the feelings, to be inconvenienced and involved, to listen with love and care. Without a willingness to risk, there will never be any real trust in the relationship—nor any real listening.

Guideline #3

Risk responding to the feelings and meaning you think you hear, rather than just the literal meaning of words. If you are wrong, at least your friend will hear you say, "I'm trying."

Listen with Your Eyes

Listening for feelings almost requires that you be able to listen with your eyes. Remember how I suggested that you visualize Paul's body and what his eyes and hands were doing? That is listening with your eyes to hear messages not expressed by words.

How many different mannerisms can you list for individual members of your family? Do they talk with their hands, pull at their hair when puzzled, drum their fingers, pick at their chins, wear certain clothes to signal a certain mood? What happens to their eyes when they're angry or hurt? How can you tell when they are nervous? Your answers to these questions will indicate how well *you* listen with your eyes.

People are constantly saying things with their bodies. Some of this information is important to hear, because although we can screen what comes out of our mouths, it's hard to shut up our bodies. Your mouth may say all is well, but the tone of your voice and your eyes may say you're miserable. Which message is more accurate? Dragging feet, pacing walk, a sigh, sweaty palms, teary eyes may be all you need to "hear" to pick up the message the other wants you to know.

A word of warning is necessary before you practice this kind of listening. People often observe an action or a mannerism and then jump to conclusions or make assumptions about what it means. The conclusions or assumptions may be wrong. Neglecting to check out the accuracy of your assumptions may result in your actually hurting someone you want to help. I was saved from doing this when I checked out an assumption.

People in an adult group were introducing themselves by talking about their names, sharing stories about what had happened to them with their names. As each talked, I observed. I noticed a young woman shifting back and forth, crossing and recrossing her legs, twiddling her thumbs, and looking at her watch. When everyone had finished and I was sharing my observations, I turned to her and carefully told her what I noticed she had been doing. Then I added, "I wondered if you were bored." She almost collapsed, letting out a deep sigh. Then she said, "Oh, I've been sitting in a chair for the past seven days, attending a seminar. I don't think I can stand to sit one more minute!" How wrong my assumption had been!

There is a psychological "law" that could have guided me in this incident. It is a law we all should remember in dealing with others. It goes this way: Never draw a profound, complex conclusion about a person's behavior unless you have first examined a simpler, more direct possible explanation. For example, don't assume that the other's behavior is due to psychological causes such as anxiety, fear, boredom, or conceit until you have first considered physical causes. These could be fatigue, hunger, pain, or illness.

You will not become a good listener with your eyes until you can completely forget yourself when you are talking to someone and can concentrate totally on the other. You have to forget worrying about whether you are "doing it right" in order to be able to see the slight twitch in the cheek muscle or the barely visible tremble of the hand. You, as the listener, must be relaxed enough to be able to listen to the words and interpret them while at the same time observing the messages of the body. This takes time to learn. It takes much practice. It takes sincere desire to learn. It takes real care and concern for the other.

Guideline #4

Observe body behaviors, facial expressions, and tone of voice for additional information the person is giving. Explore, kindly, the accuracy of this information. Even if you are mistaken, the other will know you were listening.

NOW IT'S TIME TO PRACTICE

Let's go back again to Annette, whom you met in the last chapter. She had learned about open-ended questions in her peer counseling class. She heard the "free" information about her friend's father's death. But she got anxious and reverted to what she usually did before her caring skills training—and she knew it! She needed more practice before her questioning and listening skills became useful to her in anxious, stressful situations, and a natural part of how she related to others. You probably will need practice too before these skills work for you.

In teaching these skills to peer counselors, the group setting is an advantage. Students can practice the skills on one another before they try them in their everyday social situations. For example, after demonstration and discussion of the four categories of questions one could ask (described in the last chapter), students practice using them by "interviewing" a partner about an interest. After each person in the pairs has had a turn the total group talks about what happened in each pair. Then, as part of each subsequent class session, students are asked to use open-ended questions with one another.

Students practice listening with their eyes when each has a turn to be the observer for the session. At the close of the session, the assigned observer summarizes what he or she observed and the possible meanings these observations might have regarding feelings. Often I suggest to students that whenever they have to wait someplace, such as in an airport, a restaurant, or a movie line, they practice observing people, making mental notes of what they "hear" going on.

Even though the class group does develop a trusting relationship, students *do* get nervous when they practice their skills with one another or in front of the group. But this is an important part of the practice. It helps them be more successful when they are in a real situation and become anxious.

Another advantage of the group is that the students help one another learn. Somehow it seems more powerful to hear a word of praise—or a kind suggestion made for improvement—from a classmate than from an adult teacher. Also, as students "model" the skills they are practicing, they are learning from each other. When you know your peers won't laugh at you or put you down if you make a mistake, you are freer to risk practicing what you're trying to learn.

Finally, one great advantage of the peer counseling training groups is that students discover that their peers really do care about them, that they do have similar fears and make the same mistakes. But they also see in others the changes— the progress—and they get excited! They know this is happening or can happen to them, too! They begin to believe that you *can* learn how to become a caring person.

If you don't have the opportunity to participate in a peer counseling program, why not get a group of your friends together and start working on these skills yourselves? Maybe you could get an adult you like and trust to help you do this. All of you—your friends and your adult helper—can

WHAT DO YOU HEAR?

learn together. If getting a group together isn't possible, you can still learn on your own. It may take a little longer this way, but it *can* be done. Remember, your desire to learn is the most important resource you need. Once you begin practicing the skills, you'll become more confident. As you practice, you'll discover what else you need to learn before you truly become a caring person. So now let's move on to some of these.

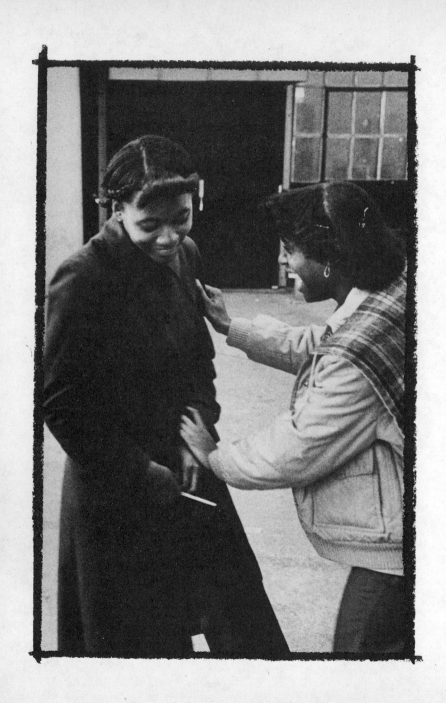

5

//////////

Come, Lonely One— Welcome

There is a species of palm tree that grows in South America called the rain tree by the natives. This tree has the power of attracting, to a wondrous degree, moisture from the air, which it condenses and drops on the earth each day as a kind of refreshing dew. The tree grows straight and green in the parched and arid desert and daily distributes its refreshing showers. The result is that around it grows an oasis of luxuriant vegetation. The rains may fail, the fountains dry up, the rivers evaporate, but the rain tree daily renews the garden that it has created about its base. Weary travelers find shade, food, a delightful rest, and new life from the gifts the tree provides.

When I first heard about these palm trees, I was moved by this miracle of nature. The more I thought about it, the more I began to wonder if it couldn't also become a miracle of *human* nature. People *are* starving and thirsty for love and friendship missing in their lives. Why couldn't you and I become human rain trees to those whose lives have become parched and barren deserts? This question developed into a plan. When I explain the details, maybe you'll get excited, too, and will want to help some lonely person by sharing daily your gifts of caring.

The plan is designed to help people who feel that they are strangers—or without any friends. These may be people your age who are new students or new neighbors; those who have no one to "go around with"; classmates who are not invited to the activities or parties; or the "odd" ones who may have a crippled body or a different color or language. Yes, the basic idea is to change how we treat individuals who are excluded or isolated from our groups. And if the plan is to succeed, it has to start with *you* and what you do or don't do to those who feel excluded when you feel comfortably secure *within* a group.

As you read this chapter, I want you to shift your thinking a little from what we've been discussing in the previous chapters. Instead of examining the skills that you need to help others, now think about your *feelings* toward others. Rather than thinking about the mistakes you might make, think about your *reasons* for giving another a helping hand. Rather than wondering about what to do, think about your *willingness* to be kind. Rather than concentrating on yourself, think about the happiness of *others*.

WE'RE ALL THE SAME INSIDE

Six students sat around the table. Two were in wheelchairs, resting their twisted, limp hands on the chair arms. One girl was wearing a leg brace. Only Cindy, the junior high student aide in this orthopedically handicapped class, had no physical disability. All the other students went to their regular schools in the morning and had special classes together in the afternoon at the orthopedic center. This afternoon they were talking about how they were treated by their classmates in their morning schools.

Tara described how she was left out of groups and made fun of by her "normal" classmates. "It's hard to make friends at that school," Tara said with emotion. Cindy nodded in agreement and told her "charges" how hard it was for her to make friends at that school when she entered last year as a new student. In her former school she had had lots of friends and been in all kinds of activities. But here, she was ignored. She admitted that even now in her second year, she often felt lonely and left out. When she finished, the group was silent. Then the teacher turned to Tara and asked her if she could explain why Cindy had the same problem making friends as she was having. Tara thought a minute and then shook her head no—but quickly added, "But I want those 'normal' kids to know that even though I might look different on the outside, I'm all the same inside."

Feelings, facts, mistaken ideas, and wisdom were expressed in that brief conversation that afternoon—all centered around loneliness and rejection. Cindy had learned the meaning of exclusion in one short year. When it first happened, she figured it was due to something that was wrong about herself. Then she decided that instead of moping around or blaming someone or the school, she would get involved in helping—so offered to be an aide in this special class. This helped her feel better about herself.

Tara, however, had known rejection all her life. She just *knew* that the reason she didn't have lots of friends was because she was disfigured. As she felt sorry for herself, she gradually became self-centered to the point where she couldn't see that others have problems too, even though they are not handicapped physically. But I will always remember what Tara said—that we're all the same inside. Despite what we look like on the outside, we all have the same inner selves that can be hurt, that need love and friendship. We all can be cruel—or kind—no matter what we're like on the outside.

You may feel like Cindy *before* she moved to a new school, a person fairly free of loneliness or rejection. Or maybe you feel more like the Cindy who now lacks friends and a group of her own. Or are you feeling like a Tara, who has never been included, thinking that others have to change before you will have friends? Wherever you are now, try momentarily to put yourself "on hold" and listen to what I have to say about loneliness and how it affects all our lives.

Loneliness, exclusion, rejection, *is* painful. If you experience this condition for long periods of time, you may lose permanently your capacity to enjoy life. This might lead to thoughts of suicide, or even to suicide itself. Loneliness is not just spending time alone. Nor is it not having enough friends. It is the feeling and fear of being a nonbeing—of feeling worthless, unwanted. Loneliness was the most commonly mentioned and most intensely felt of the five cries reported in the book I mentioned in the first chapter, *The Five Cries of Youth.* Eighty-seven percent of the youth in that study said that outside their families they really belonged to no group and were bothered by the lack of friends at school.

If you have experienced loneliness, or are lonely now, you know what I am saying. Excluded from a group, avoided at parties or never even asked, you begin to hate yourself. You begin to feel ugly and undesirable when you're around others. Cliff Evans was lonely. He kept hearing the voices saying, "You're a nothing."

Loneliness, however, is a condition that can't be changed without the help of others. We can change lots of things ourselves. We can learn the skills of making conversations and listening. We can learn how to make friends. But there is no way to make a group accept you or me. Welcoming another, including him or her, must voluntarily come from those inside the group, from individuals who care enough about the feelings of others. Knowing this, it seems especially cruel to see people who were once lonely or outside themselves turn away from helping another who is being excluded. In fact, some even lead the way in rejecting or ignoring the lonely Cliff Evanses who are around them.

We were having a class election in my eighth-grade social studies class, and those who had been nominated were waiting outside for the votes to be counted. As they returned, Dave jeeringly yelled at Tim, "No one voted for *you,* Tim." Challenged by me for such a cruel remark, Dave admitted that he was only trying to get even. In the past, he had always been the one to be hurt—to be taunted. Now he had a chance to do the same to someone else. It didn't matter to him that Tim had never hurt him. He was just an innocent victim. He wanted to hurt *anyone,* because he had been hurt so often. How sad! In doing this, he was now hurting himself even more than he hurt Tim.

Have you been hurt by a group? Have you ever walked alone, watching a group up ahead ignore you? Have you stood with students who were laughing about something, but didn't tell *you* what was funny? If you have, then you know what it feels like to be a stranger—an outsider. You also know how helpless you are in trying to *make* a group include you. The welcome, the invitation, must come from someone within.

When a group accepts a new person, most often it is because *someone* had the courage to be kind; was willing to take the lead; cared more about the feelings of the one excluded than about protecting his or her own place in the group. Strangely enough, such a person is one whom the group silently admires and respects.

The incident happened one rainy morning on the campus of a suburban high school. It was a school that had more than its share of cliques. Every brunch, students would stand around the center quad, clustered in these cliques, talking and eyeing whatever was going on. Anyone who wanted to go to the other side of the quad, to avoid calling attention to him- or herself, would walk *around* the quad, rather than using the shorter route across it.

In the midst of this mid-morning ritual, a fairly heavy, somewhat unattractive girl started across the quad, intent on getting to the opposite corner. Clearly she *had* to be a new student because she didn't know the rules! She was carrying a load of books. About midpoint, she slipped and fell spread-eagled on the pavement, her books scattering in all directions. Immediately, a roar of laughter and put-downs arose from the spectators all around. Then suddenly, John, a nice-looking boy, a member of the "jock" group, started walking slowly out to the girl. Expectant silence fell. When he reached her, he bent down and began picking up her books, then helped her up. Not a sound came from anyone, even when John and his companion reached her destination. Slowly the crowd dispersed.

What would *you* have done if you had been part of the group that day and had seen the girl fall? What might have been your fears about doing what John did? Why might you be afraid? What if it had been one of *your* friends who ventured out to help this girl, what would have been your thoughts or feelings? Do you have any friends who might have the courage to risk the ridicule of most of the student body and act in such a caring way? Why didn't the crowd boo and laugh at John? Maybe they didn't because he was a "jock"; maybe they didn't because he was nice-looking. I believe they didn't because they were moved by this compassionate act and felt ashamed of their own lack of courage. Perhaps next time, one or two others may have the desire and the will to follow John's example.

I believe many of you *do* want to act as John did. I think that you *do* want to learn how to say through your actions, "Come lonely, rejected, ridiculed, made-fun-of boy or girl—welcome." If you do, let's explore further what keeps us from extending a caring welcome to another.

I DIDN'T WANT TO HURT YOU

Learning how to welcome a stranger to a group is one of the caring skills taught in peer counseling. The teaching activity is designed to simulate what happens when a group "welcomes" a stranger and to illustrate the difference between kind welcomes and cruel ones. As students become involved in the simulation, each one begins to reveal how she or he might in fact act when faced with a real opportunity to include someone into a group. What happens in these practice exercises often is a startling revelation to the students. A brief description of the activity will help you understand what I mean.

The group is divided into small groups of six or seven in number. Each group then selects one of its members to take the role of stranger. This person leaves the room while the rest decide what kind of a group it will be—a club, a youth group, or neighborhood friends. When this is decided, they discuss how they will welcome their "stranger"—the strategies they will use. When they have a plan, the group brings their stranger in and proceeds with the "welcoming." After a short period of time, each group is asked to stop, and the total group gathers to discuss what happened.

A group of youth leaders in Los Angeles had just completed this whole simulation and were sitting talking about the experience, looking somber and confused. B. J. sat hunched over, his head in his hands. He had been selected as the stranger in this group. He had pleaded not to have to take this role, but his group had insisted. Waiting in the hall to be called back in, it was obvious he was scared. When he finally was called in, the group told him he was a new member of their youth club. That was all. Then the attack began. It started with, "We don't want you here. You'd break up our group. Why do you want to come in with us? What do *you* have to offer to us?" Quietly, Dolores tried to intrude, saying, "I don't think that's what we're supposed to be doing . . . ," but her comment was drowned out by the gradually increasing jeers and volume of their voices. Shocked, not believing what I was seeing and hearing, I called a halt. Now sobered by the results of their "fun," each one seemed confused. Some didn't know what they had done wrong. Some said, "I didn't want to hurt you." But they had. It hurt so much, B. J. seemed to be in shock.

Why and how did this happen? Was this just an isolated incident with a group of cruel young people? No, they weren't basically cruel. Nor was it just an isolated accident. Sadly, I have witnessed many other groups treat their chosen stranger in similar ways.

It happened in this case because these youth didn't know *how* to make someone feel welcome. They were doing just what they knew based on how they had been treated by others. Later, after repeating the activity again to do it "right," one girl said, "It's really *hard* to be nice to someone." She was finding it a struggle to learn how to be kind.

Since that day I have found that many people don't know the skills of being kind and welcoming to a new person who comes to a group. Instead, in this exercise they sometimes ask the newcomer one question after another. Sometimes the group checks out the person's past achievements or credentials, asking whom they know and what they have done and other personal questions. Some groups almost smother the person with invitations or requests for help. As the "stranger" tells the group afterwards how he or she was affected by their methods, some are horrified by what they have done. Some sadly confess, "We didn't want to hurt you."

THE "WHYS" OF WHAT WE DO

When anyone makes the confession that he or she didn't deliberately hurt the stranger, another question often follows: "Why did I do it?" Some realize that they saw what was happening but didn't know what to do or say to stop it. Why?

I Am Confused About the Meaning of Welcome. The most common reason, and the one that can be most easily forgiven, is that people don't know the real meaning of welcome. Do you? Are you *sure?* I ask, for the simple reason that the meaning of welcome has to be experienced before it is understood. If the only "welcomes" you have experienced have been difficult or unpleasant, such as Cindy's was in her new school, then it is possible that you understand welcome as a negative introduction into a new group.

The word actually means "to please another well; to be received gladly into one's presence or companionship; the giving of pleasure." How many times have you been received this way when you were a stranger? Probably not often, if you are like the many others who have answered this question. Therein lies the confusion about the way to offer a welcome.

Shirley found no one who was friendly. Instead boys pulled her hair, ripped her books, and made fun of her. Annette was new in the seventh grade. She wasn't picked on—just ignored. Charles, too, was ignored, and it wasn't until he became a star athlete that he began to get some friends. Now Shirley, Annette, and Charles find it hard to reach out to others spontaneously. Their negative treatment by groups has made them feel fearful of groups. It even has made them afraid to offer a warm hello to others. Memories are powerful barriers that can limit what we let ourselves do. It's hard to reach out to another if one has never experienced a sincere, warm welcome.

Ignorance is only a partial answer to the question "Why did I do it?" There are other reasons; here are two more of them.

I Am Thoughtless About Everybody Else. Perhaps one of the main reasons we are unkind to those outside the group is because we are selfish. Enjoying the company of friends, engrossed in what is going on, we just don't want to bother with bringing someone new in. It takes effort. It means we have to stop what we are doing to include the new girl or boy in our "in" stories, jokes, and activities.

But the basic problem we face in welcoming someone is

our thoughtlessness. We just don't think about it. We aren't alert to another's presence or need. We don't think how our casualness might make a stranger feel. And *that* is being thoughtless. We aren't deliberately trying to hurt. But we don't stop to think how the comments, silences, or lack of recognition might seem unfriendly. Maybe the person didn't look that important, or that interesting. Thoughtlessness can be as brutal as teasing or jesting, because the person who is the target feels like a nothing.

I Don't Trust Myself. Many of the unkind words or acts of others, especially those of young people, have been excused by attributing them to insecurity. No one wants to admit he or she is insecure, but often we hide behind its skirts to cover our negative behavior. For example, some might say Dave's words to Tim about the election were because Dave was insecure. This is supposed to mean that Dave really didn't mean what he was saying.

This may be true. Perhaps Dave didn't mean it. Over half of the young people (52 percent) in the *Five Cries* study said that they behave differently in a group. Half of these 7,050 students also said they feel pressure at school to do what others do. When you act differently than you are for self-protection, at the expense of another, that *is* insecurity. It may not be what you do that hurts, but what you don't do—for example, remaining silent when others are jeering or hurting. Silently protecting yourself, you unwillingly contribute to the loneliness and hurt of another. Many of you want to be free of this insecurity. You want to develop both self-respect and the courage to respond to that inner self when courage is needed.

Alice was the weirdest girl in school. As my peer counseling group met each week, her name always came up, accompanied by laughter and a story about the latest dumb thing she had done. She wore strange combinations of clothes. She barged into a group to stand by someone she knew. She yelled out your name as you walked down the hall, getting everyone to look at you—and her! She even wrote a "love" note to one of my group saying how much she liked her and wanted to be her friend. Showing me the note, Jennifer screwed up her face and said, "Only *kids* do stuff like that."

Determined that these eighth-grade girls were going to help Alice, I began to "motivate" them. I suggested more constructive ways each could handle the awkward, embarrassing situations Alice created. For example, when they saw her in the halls, they could quickly go up to her *before* she had a chance to scream or yell to them. Why not invite her to join them for lunch? Or Betty could choose her as her practice partner in drama. The group began thinking that *I* was weird—knowing it would be impossible to do these things. But I kept talking, and gradually I heard fewer negative stories about Alice. Instead, I began hearing that Alice was changing. She was dressing more neatly; she had quieted down; she was making some friends; some of the girls had even invited her to their homes and done some things with her after school. The girls had started thinking about what was happening to Alice and in doing so had found the courage to risk ridicule themselves by being seen with her and being nice to her. They actually became "rain trees" for Alice, providing a source of now life for her. As they did, they also grew more secure and confident themselves—and more caring.

The important message in the story of Alice is that these girls overcame their own insecurity by helping someone else who needed them. Try it yourself. As soon as you stop feeling sorry for yourself and dwelling on *your* inadequacies and begin concentrating on the needs of others, you too will find you like and trust yourself much more.

HE TURNED AWAY

It isn't always easy. You will find people who *are* hard to welcome. They are those who appear aloof, who sometimes lash out with ugly remarks, who apparently are not "long-ing thirstily" for your kindness or company. Even when in-vited to come into your friendship circle, they turn away. These are people who are so lonely, who feel so unworthy, that *they are afraid to trust your offers of friendship.* Peo-ple have been phony before. They have been hurt by ges-tures that were shallow or dishonest. They need to have you prove that *you* can be trusted. So they test you. They won't help you to be kind. It's like a starving traveler who won't come into the shade of the rain tree, fearing a snake might strike or that the food will be poisoned.

Nancy Nelson, a seventeen-year-old-girl, put it in these words:

> Standing apart
> I heard you say hello
> It was sweet of you to try
> but I was (after all)
> standing apart.
> (*Five Cries of Youth*, p. 21)

She heard you say hello but stayed apart, finally turning away.

Maybe this was because you didn't call again. Maybe a second or third call was needed to prove that you meant it. Could it be that in the past Nancy had experienced exclu-sions, attacks of gossip, slurs, and jokes, to the point where she was hesitant about your greeting or invitation? It may not be that Nancy does not trust *you*. She may find it hard to trust anyone, or any group.

One group doing the "welcoming" activity convinced me that such feelings are very common. After all the "strangers" were selected by their small groups, I joined them in the hall. They approached me and said, "We've decided we aren't go-ing back in there. We are going to be a group of our own. We don't need *them*." These were adults saying this. They were half-heartedly laughing as they told me what they planned to do. But eventually, they did go back and face what awaited them in the various ways they were welcomed.

The message of what they had said, though, hit me. People who are pushed out and treated as rejects *do* find other lonely strangers to be their companions. When they do, they turn their backs on the "in" groups. Why go back and take the chance of being hurt again? So, of course, they may rebuff our welcomes and refuse our invitations. But, can we look beneath that surface protection, hiding fear and distrust, and say yet another time, perhaps in a different way—"Come, I truly want you as a friend?"

Are you one who stands apart? If you are, *please listen!* The price is high. If you give up trying to find a true friendship, it can make you bitter and emotionally numb. You may believe it is what you have to do to survive. But in the end, you may find yourself only *existing*, rather than living. Others have been hurt but have not given up. They have gone back again and again to find the one friend who will welcome them. They do this because they know they need the food of human relationships to live.

This is what Strommen is talking about in *Five Cries of Youth* (p. 21):

> The issue is not so much friends, as the ability to commit oneself to another. To know the trust of deep attachments a young person must entrust himself to others. Inability to do so robs him of the affection which he needs so desperately. Unable to open his life to others in a caring and loving way, he does not experience the love and affection of others which could give him a sense of well-being and worth.

Think about this. Even if you have all the friends you want, read the quote again. Think about what commitment means and about the kind of trust you give and get back. How often do you keep your real feelings hidden because you're afraid of your friends' reaction—afraid to trust what they will do? If you keep on hiding those feelings, you will find eventually you're cut off from any deep attachments. Then you've lost a precious gift of life. You can't love or be attached to someone without the chance that you'll be hurt. If you do love another and are hurt, you still will have known what love is. If you decide to never get involved with a commitment of your feelings, you won't get hurt, but what does it matter? What makes life most satisfying—experiencing love, or avoiding pain? We have to decide, because we don't seem able to have both.

A CHECKLIST OF WHAT TO DO

When you were in grade school, perhaps your teacher sometimes pinned a note on your sweater reminding you to bring back a health card or milk money—or to give a message to your mother. It worked—you remembered—or the teacher wouldn't have done it.

The suggestions I'm going to give you are reminders of what to do when you have a chance to welcome someone. Don't write them out and pin them on your coat, though! Instead, pin them on your mind and heart so they will prick you into action. Use the memory of B. J., Tim, Alice, and others as your safety pin. Think about them and what *your* actions might mean to someone who has been pushed out or left out.

These reminders vary in usefulness depending on the situation or the person needing the welcome. Some are effective with including new students; some are directions for assisting someone who is picked on; others apply to acquaintances who are handicapped or visibly different. To help you decide which method to use for what person or situation, put yourself in the place of the other person. Ask how you would like to be treated. Then act.

1. Use Food to Show Warmth

The best understood language of friendliness is the offer of food or drink. A plate of cookies or a soft drink has often greased the awkward wheels of conversation among strangers. Partly this is so because it provides people with something to do if they can't think of anything to say.

Adults often use food too, as an icebreaker for getting acquainted. Has your mother ever taken a casserole or cake to a new neighbor as a friendly way of introducing herself? Neighbors are sometimes invited to a coffee to initiate a neighborhood introduction. You'd probably feel dumb taking a casserole to the boy who just moved in next door. But you could invite him for lunch or treat him to a soft drink after school. And he really might appreciate an invitation to dinner at your home and a chance to see you with your family. Just watch the next new girl in your youth group relax when you meet her at the door and walk her over to the refreshment table! Food can be your helper in reaching out your hand to say hello.

2. Stretch Out Your Hand

There are huge differences in how sincere you seem, depending on which parts of your body you use. For example: A new boy arrives at your backpacking club. You notice him. You say, "Hi," and that's all. Or—you gesture for him to come over and join you and wait to see if he does. Or—you walk over, say "hi," invite him to join you, and walk with him as you go to your place in the group. If you were an adult, you might also offer your hand when you say "hi"—but that may be too formal. Which one of these welcomes would *you* want? My guess is you'd like being met, invited to join, and accompanied across the room.

When you stop and think about it, isn't it awful the way we treat new people when they come to a group for the first time? Imagine what it is like for the person who appears at the door and enters, only to have everyone stop talking. All eyes seem riveted on the person standing alone. It's amazing that more people don't just turn around and leave. It only takes one such experience to make a person fear or dread the next new group he or she has to enter. Some handle such awkward moments by taking the initiative. They approach someone nearby and start a conversation by introducing themselves. This takes self-confidence! Most people just remain silent, sitting or standing alone, until someone notices—if anybody ever does. Save others this misery. Stretch out your hand by doing something to include them.

3. Turn Off the Spotlight

I'll bet you don't enjoy standing in a circle, being the center of attention for people you don't know, while they quiz you about yourself. If you're a celebrity, this may be nice. But if you're the stranger, how does it feel? Awful! You get nervous, maybe hear yourself blabbering more than you want to, or develop a strong urge to escape.

If this makes *you* feel uncomfortable, why not do something to turn off the spotlight when it's focused on someone else. Try turning the attention to others by questioning *them*. Volunteer some information about yourself. Get the group talking to one another. It is much easier to meet one or two people at a time rather than having to take on a whole group at once. Anyone has a better chance to relax and carry on a conversation when faced with one or two rather than the whole group. Another way to eliminate the spotlight is to get a new person involved in the group activity. If nothing else works, you could say, "Hey, let's knock it off and let Ken relax his vocal cords." Ken probably will offer you a silent thank-you.

Sometimes the spotlight treatment feels like an admission interview. Even though your questions are meant to show an interest, they can sound like a qualifying exam. What if the new girl doesn't want to go to college, or the new guy hates sports because his body hasn't developed yet, or her father delivers mail? Do they flunk your "exam"?

We forget something important when we try to welcome with a series of rapid-fire "interested" questions. We forget that newcomers are not beggars. People like to pick and choose their groups, and to do this they want information, too. They want to know something about those in the group, as well as being checked out *by* the group. So remember this: Move slowly. Give the person some space—and some information about yourself—before you ask too many "interested" questions.

4. Volunteer Directions or Other Useful Information

Finding out where places are and how to get there is the first need and challenge to a newcomer. Take the rest rooms, for example. Sometimes it isn't obvious where they are, and it is often embarrassing to ask. Jim said he went a whole week in a new school before he found them—he was afraid to ask. Save a new student the embarrassment and anticipate what he or she might want to know. It's better to tell too much than too little. Volunteer some of the in-jokes of the school or the quirks of the teachers. Warn a new student that Mrs. Temper throws fits if you come late to class or that the janitor throws away everything left behind in the classroom. Sure, this isn't vital information, but it *does* help a person feel as if he or she is more on the "inside." It can save awkward situations and help the person feel more relaxed. With a little thought, I'm sure you'll know what kind of information will do the job.

These first four suggestions are fairly low-risk things to do to help a newcomer. They will probably be easy for you to do, if you just think about them. Sometimes, however, a person needs a welcome that requires courage and effort. The ones who do are the lonely ones who don't fit in easily with a group. They are the Alices and B.J.'s—your classmates who may be excluded from normal peer activities because they are physically or mentally handicapped. Are you *willing* to care enough to do what I am going to suggest in numbers 5 and 6 on the checklist.

5. Make an Attempt to Rescue

Remember what the group did to B. J.? If Dolores had *shouted,* "Stop it!" if she had demanded to be heard, B. J.

might have been rescued. He might have been only bruised by their words rather than hurt the way he was.

Betty and Jennifer and the others could have ignored suggestions to help Alice, not wanting to pay the price of possible ridicule for associating with the school scapegoat. But they did. They rescued Alice from the cruel treatment she was getting from others. As they did, they earned the satisfaction of seeing the results they accomplished.

Dolores missed her opportunity because she wasn't prepared—she didn't know what to do. Betty and Jennifer and Liz didn't know either, until they learned and practiced what they were taught. You can learn, too, and if you apply what we've been discussing, you too will see results. But don't anticipate appreciation. Expect only some private satisfaction in knowing what you have done. Rescues can be done with only a word, a sentence, or a refusal to join in with the laughter and put-downs targeted at defenseless people. It takes courage. You have to be *willing* to do it.

6. Take on the Tough Ones

Kevin's eyes are crossed and his head jerks back when he talks. It's hard to feel comfortable around him. You don't like looking at him and feel almost ashamed of your own healthy, well-coordinated body. If you are with him, you don't know what to say or do. Should you wait for Kevin as he limps along or walk ahead? Should you offer to carry his books? Or should you just ignore him?

Melissa's eyes are dull. Her coordination is awful. When you try talking to her, she laughs in the wrong places or blabbers away on some thought of her own. Who would want her for a friend? But even though she's mentally retarded, she *is* sweet and loving. Too much so, at times. She often wants to hug you, no matter who is around! How could you *really* try to be a friend to her? Your conscience does bother you when kids make fun of her. Sometimes you wonder how she must hurt inside, or if she is ever happy.

Susan is a burnout. She smokes pot regularly and often gets stoned on weekends. Her clothes are sloppy. She skips classes. She smokes with the group on the hill. She also makes crude remarks to you and your friends. Help *her?* Instead, act as though she didn't exist! She doesn't need a friend. She doesn't want my help. Or does she . . . ?

Who could be more lonely than those who are physically, mentally, emotionally, or socially handicapped or disabled? They are pushed aside for many reasons. But they don't want pity—not even Kevin. They want to be accepted! Pity makes them inferior. They want to be treated as equals.

For the Kevins, Melissas, and Susans, caring is a *real* gift. It is, because you have to see beyond the deformed body, the dwarfed mind, and the destructive behavior to find the lonely person within. If you are willing to help, ask professional people who work with these young people what you could or should do to show you care about them. Your ability to help starts with your willingness to try.

WHAT YOU EXPECT IN RETURN

A phony welcome can hurt more deeply than none at all. Since we all are tempted to give this kind of welcome, I want to remind you of this. It is so easy to fool ourselves. The "do-gooder" attitude is a powerful put-down. It implies the superiority of the giver, who is more "together" than the one who is welcomed. The "strings-attached" gift is a cheap way of getting what you want or making yourself feel important. We probably all have some "I-am-good" thoughts when we do something for another. However, a *caring* person needs to check periodically on what he or she expects in return for the help.

Certainly most people expect appreciation in return for help. If you are genuinely friendly to a new student, it's pretty natural to expect some thanks. Sometimes a group expects to "own" a new member in exchange for him or her being included. It also seems normal to expect some help yourself when you need it from one you have treated kindly.

Often these expectations are not met. They aren't for a number of reasons. Probably the main reason is that many people don't know how to say thank you. They feel appreciation but are embarrassed to show any kind of gratitude. They don't know how to "do it right." Some are silent with their thanks because they aren't sure you'll know they *mean* it—that you won't think it's just a bunch of empty words.

What this all adds up to is this: Caring must be given without any strings attached. Assume that the other does appreciate what you have done. Model showing appreciation to them, when you have an opportunity. Give them what you wish they would give to you.

So in summary, here are your reminder notes to pin on your memory:

1. *Use food to show warmth* by initiating a friendship over lunch or the refreshment table.
2. *Stretch out your hand* by going more than halfway in efforts to welcome the other.
3. *Turn off the spotlight* by shifting attention away from the newcomer.
4. *Volunteer directions or useful information* to help a new person feel less awkward or "new."
5. *Make an attempt to rescue* by helping someone who is put-down or ignored.
6. *Take on the tough ones* by responding to their silent cries for help.

THE RAIN TREE YOU CAN BE

Three out of four of the young people who admitted they were lonely in the *Five Cries* study said they wanted to be part of a caring, accepting group. A majority of those who said this also said they wanted a group whose members, in addition to offering acceptance, also confronted one another with an honest sharing of personal feelings. These young people wanted to be part of groups that allowed them to be who they are without fear of evaluation or rejection. These groups would be ones that truly welcomed the lonely ones.

These young people were not asking for groups that had had special training or certain skills. They were asking to be with people who are accepting and warm, who can help someone feel good about her- or himself. *You* can be that kind of person and give that kind of help without training— if you want to.

Remember the rain trees I talked about at the beginning of this chapter? Each one of you, no matter what you're like today, could be a human rain tree to your companions who want to be part of a caring, accepting group. By doing the things we've talked about, you could change a group so that it becomes a human oasis for some of the hurting, lonely students in your school, community, or church. Just as the palm trees miraculously attract moisture from the atmosphere, such a group could supply kindness and concern for others from the goodness within you. The miracle is that the love or care you give to others will never run dry. In fact, you'll find love returned to you the more you give away. It can all start with you. You don't have to wait for others to join you before you can begin reaching out to lonely people. Just look around you and decide where and when you're going to begin.

Others may not believe you can do it—that you and your friends *are* willing to use your lives as rain trees of love for others. These are those who only expect negative or selfish acts from young people. But peer counseling students have shown it *is* possible. These students *have* become a shelter for lonely peers. In doing so, they have found their own lives are less lonely; they feel like more worthwhile people.

6

////////////

What Do
I Do After
I've Listened?

In the last chapter, I wrote about loneliness and some of the things you could do to relieve the loneliness of others. But this is not the only reason why a friend is needed. Sometimes a person has a problem or a decision to make or is confused and can't figure out what to do. In situations like this a pet, a car, or even your favorite book won't help. You need someone you can turn to for help, or who at least will listen with understanding, someone you trust. *You* may be that someone! Or you may want to be that someone. If one of your friends does come to you seeking help, you want to be prepared; you need to know how to help—after you've listened. That's the topic we'll explore now.

If you want to be successful in helping someone with a problem you have to know the process of helping—the broad picture of what you're trying to do. Understanding what is involved also equips you to deal with your own problems. If I can assume you realize this, then I can simplify what I'm going to be telling you by focusing only on your approach when someone comes to you with a problem, asking for help. This is what we call "counseling" our friends. To be an effective "counselor-friend" you need the skills we've covered in the previous chapters. But you also need to understand *what* you're trying to do—what is helpful and what isn't.

Young people have many real problems—problems meeting the expectations of parents, teachers, society, and a constantly changing self. Your bodies are developing and changing; boy-girl relationships are confusing to you, or you have a problem because you don't have a boyfriend or girlfriend. Some of you are uncertain about what you want or what you value. Career decisions are getting serious, and each young person faces the decision whether to get married, live with someone, or remain single. One moment a young person feels restricted by his or her parents, the next moment, is angry because parents aren't sufficiently firm. Some struggle with deciding on religious beliefs, philosophy of life, or moral and ethical standards. It's hard work becoming a mature adult, and in the process anyone can run into a snag. That's when a person needs an objective, but caring, friend to help.

At this age it seems natural to turn to a friend who is going through the same thing, who has similar struggles and doubts, who is as much in the dark about the future as you are. These friends know your problems are serious and don't tell you not to worry, or that you'll grow out of it, as many parents do. Friends can share with each other, entrusting to friendship what few others understand or know.

Just talking about a problem can help. But sometimes as you pour out your problems, you get a feeling the friend doesn't understand, doesn't hear the feelings behind your words. If you are the listener trying to understand, you may not be sure what to say or do. Being anxious to help, you may give some advice, based on something you saw on TV, read in a book, or tried yourself. When you've finished, though, you're not sure you've helped, or that the advice was all that good. So what *can* you do after you've listened?

Charlie Brown's Lucy may have ready answers to that question; most young people don't. Many students have asked, "How do I really help my friends with their problems?" I'd like to help you and others find an answer to that question. What I'm going to tell you is what I teach students in peer counseling. I practice these principles myself as a professional counselor. I believe these are suggestions that can help you respond effectively and practically to the problems of your friends, as well as the ones you face yourself. If you practice them enough, you will find they become your natural way of responding to others. If you want or need more detailed information about counseling and human relationship skills, read some of the books that have been written on this subject. I have included a list of some of the better ones at the end of this book.

THE ONES YOU TURN TO FOR HELP

Most people are fortunate to have been touched by some person or persons in significant and positive ways at different times in their lives. Many can say, with honesty, that a father or mother has been such a person. But often the ones we remember best with real thanks, and who influenced our lives most vividly, were those who helped us just because they cared about us—not because they were supposed to care, but because they wanted to care. Could you name one or two people like that who have been important in your life? Let's do an exercise that I ask students to do in class.

1. Get a piece of paper and a pencil. Then sit for several minutes thinking about people who have been in your life—uncles, teachers, pastors, coaches, anyone you feel helped to change your life in some meaningful and constructive way.
2. Take your time—but after you remember who these people are, write on your paper their names and what each one did that was so important to you.
3. When you have finished, go back over the list and think

about the qualities these people had or have and make a list of them on your paper.

4. Looking at your list, ask yourself how you would rate yourself on these qualities.

5. Then ask yourself how helpful you have been to others. If some of your friends or members of your family were doing this exercise, would they put you on their list? Don't be modest—think honestly about this question.

6. Finally, write down answers to the question, What unique qualities do I think I have that might contribute to my being a helpful person? Please—don't read further before you have done this.

In my classes, students don't write this exercise, but rather talk about their "significant" person, telling the group about him or her. As they do, their faces seem to soften, or they sometimes cry as they reflect and remember. Few have nothing to say.

After each person has shared, we make a list of the qualities mentioned. From the list we develop a kind of profile of the kinds of people we might turn to for help with a problem. One vivid theme that is mentioned repeatedly is: "He (or she) paid attention to me—or noticed me, or saw something good in me—when I was feeling worthless, ugly, dirty, or at rock bottom." Another way of saying it is that these people saw another's need and helped, with no strings attached, even when it wasn't expected or requested. Some say that this person continued to show an interest and volunteer help despite a lack of response or evidence of appreciation. "He believed in me, and eventually I began to like and accept myself, too" is often their concluding summary.

You might be interested in other frequently mentioned qualities. Here is a sampling: "Gave me time when he didn't have to" • "Taught me different ways to deal with conflict" • "Did not judge me" • "Took my side and understood my point of view" • "Recognized that my feelings were very important" • "Showed me different ways of understanding a person" • "Believed in me and gave me confidence" • "Showed an interest in me and pointed out alternatives" • "Helped me to risk trust and openness."

As students talk about these qualities they often agree that a necessary requirement for someone they would turn to for help is that this person be honest and open. They frequently disagree about whether this is a skill one learns or whether it just takes guts. As Tammi said, "It seems like people are just waiting for someone to be honest, so they can be honest right back. One person has to take the risk when you're dealing with feelings before somebody else is willing to do the same with you."

Many people are not open and honest because they go through life "wearing their raincoats in the shower." All of us want to be loved, to be able to express feelings without fear of censure, to bind companionship with natural and spontaneous interactions. But we often keep it from happening by being buttoned-up people. We stand in the shower with raincoats buttoned up to our chins—not letting our inner self be shared and exposed to the richness and the cleansing of human relationships. Those who are willing to take off those raincoats are the open and honest ones we want to find—as helpers and as friends.

Many students who start peer counseling are not open and honest. All vary in the qualities they have for being effective "counselors." But they all want to improve. It is interesting that some who feel they have the least to offer and need the most help develop the greatest sensitivity and effectiveness in helping others. If you want to be the kind of friend to whom someone would turn for help, come with me.

RATING YOURSELF

To begin, you need to rate yourself, so you will know where you need or want to improve. Here is a suggested list of qualities you might value in a friend and might want to have yourself. Carefully read through the list. Think about each one and evaluate yourself, using specific examples. Then go back through the list. This time, mark a rating of yourself after each item. Use the following code:

S — You're satisfied that you have this quality.
NEED — You feel a need to improve on this quality.
? — You aren't sure. You don't know.

The exercise will be useful only if you are completely honest. This means you have to admit to yourself that you *do* have good qualities. If some are marked "NEED," ask yourself why you think you need to improve. Do the same with those marked with question marks. The list probably is not complete, so think of other qualities you feel are equally or more important. Add these to the list and rate them along with the others.

Since this kind of self-rating is very personal, it would be a good idea for you to do this on a separate sheet. Put the title at the top. Then list each item, for example, "Like People," and your rating next to the item. This way no one will see it, and you can refer to it often.

RATING HELPING QUALITIES

_____ 1. Like people: At times you feel socially awkward, but you basically like to be with people and are curious about them.

_____ 2. Respect and trust others: You not only like people, but you also value them and respect their worth. Your first reaction usually is to trust others and believe in their good intentions.

_____ 3. Are able to accept the faults of others: You can value the person despite behavior you may dislike. You don't reject someone because of his or her faults. You try to understand and give help, if asked.

_____ 4. Can express your own feelings: You can be honest and open, when it is appropriate, about what you feel about yourself, others, or the situation. You express these feelings kindly and directly.

_____ 5. Are able to admit your own problems and faults: You realize you aren't perfect. You can acknowledge your problems. You don't hide your faults from others or yourself. You work to correct these faults.

_____ 6. Are in touch with what you value: Although you feel your values may be changing, you think you know what is important to you now and are willing to commit yourself publicly.

_____ 7. Are willing to inconvenience yourself for others: You'd give up a game with friends or a favorite TV program to help someone. You'll listen for the seventh time to the same story if telling it makes the other person feel better.

_____ 8. Don't get kicks out of another's hurt: You don't make fun of another or label others or use put-downs that might hurt or pressure another to do as you wish.

_____ 9. Can be trusted with a confidence: What is shared about personal matters is honored, no matter who else has been told. You don't gossip and casually use information about others.

_____10. Other: (Write in other qualities you value in a person you would turn to for help.)

Keep this list. Review it and possibly revise it later, checking to see what progress you may be making in achieving the qualities you desire.

WHICH WAY SHOULD I GO FROM HERE?

Developing these qualities is a beginning. Next, you need to know how to proceed if and when someone *does* turn to you for help.

When Alice was roaming around in Wonderland, she came to a crossroads where she met the Cheshire Cat. She said to him, "Would you tell me, please, which way I ought to go from here?" What the cat replied will come later.

Asking which way to go from here is another way of asking, "What should I do about my problem?" It's nice to be asked. You are complimented that someone thinks you know the way. What do you say? How do you answer?

A class spent time discussing the answer to these two questions. The discussion started with a fantasy described by the teachers and ended with an attempt to define what is meant by "counseling." As students listened to the fantasy, they were asked to be aware of their reactions and feelings. Briefly, this is what the class was told:

The adults in the community had gotten together and come up with a plan that they knew would benefit young people. Observing how teenagers live, it was obvious they were doing a poor job of making their own decisions. They ate too much junk food, played crummy music, and chose lousy friends. So the adults were going to take over and from now on would make all the decisions for students. Since they had more experience and had learned a lot from their own mistakes during adolescence, the adults knew this would help young people avoid making the same mistakes. Adults were willing to listen to any objections to this plan before they put it into operation. However, they would only listen to rational reasons why the plan wouldn't work. Emotional objections would be rejected. If any student had ideas why the plan wouldn't work, now was the time to express them.

Without losing a second, the class began to react—giving both rational *and* emotional reasons why this plan would be a disaster. Here's a portion of what the students said:

David: Part of the pleasure of having friends is choosing them and seeing if they are like you and have the same interests as you do. How would teachers know that about someone and be able to choose my friends for me?

Elke: Also, how are you ever going to become an adult knowing how to make decisions if you can't make them when you're young?

Lisa: We would become so dependent on you adults that we wouldn't be able to do anything. We'd have to have you around all the time, like bodyguards.

Karen: Yeah, like you said you'd choose the music we'd listen to . . . that would be the music *you* want to listen to, not the music we want to listen to.

Annie: So we do make mistakes—so what? That's the way we learn. If everybody told you everything, you wouldn't know, and like if you were away from your parents, you wouldn't know much . . . you have to learn for yourself.

Would you agree with what these students were saying? You *are* more informed about your decisions than any other person. Only you can know the kind of friends you want. You do need the freedom to make mistakes so that you can learn from them. No one could possibly know you well enough to make all your decisions in a way that would make you happy.

This class discussion relates to how you might answer the question "What should I do about my problems?" If you tell the person what he or she should do, it is the same as making a decision for him or her. Your advice may be harmful for all the reasons these students gave in objecting to the plan in the fantasy. These students agreed it was much better to help people make their own decisions. David thought you could do this by kind of walking them through what they should do, looking at the goods and the bads. But eventually, the person must decide on his or her own what to do about the problem.

As the class discussion continued, they eventually began trying to define the difference between *counseling* and *sympathy*—or "cheering someone up." What's unique about "counseling" another?

"'Cheering up' is what they really want to hear," Sharon said.

"Sympathy can make a person feel worse. It sometimes is agreeing with the person," Elke thought.

"When you sympathize with people, they are at the same place they were when they came to you. Counseling is going someplace else," David contributed.

"Counseling is more like listening and looking at the facts," Karen thought.

"I guess counseling is just like pulling it out of the person . . ." David added.

Counseling—or helping—then, means listening to people; allowing them to express themselves; helping them to look at alternatives and at the consequences of those alternatives; helping people make their own decisions. Counseling is being warm and keeping confidences. It's not giving sympathy. It's not giving advice. And it's not just "cheering up."

This seems like a fairly big task; but when you sort it out, it basically requires the skills we have already talked about. It involves asking questions, listening, being concerned about the feelings of others, genuinely wanting to help— and being the kind of person *you* would want as a friend.

A wise seventh-grade student said it better. When asked *his* definition of counseling, he said: "Counseling is helping others give advice to themselves."

THE ANSWERS YOU MIGHT GIVE

Let's go back to Alice in Wonderland, whom we left hanging with her question of what path she ought to take from there. The Cheshire Cat answered with another question: "Where do you want to get to?" Alice replied, "I don't much care where." So the Cat told her that in that case, it didn't matter which path she took.

The Cat obviously knew the first step in helping others give advice to themselves. That first step is guiding a person to declare where he or she wants to go or assisting a friend to describe the problem. Eventually, when a person is able to tell you what it is he or she wants changed or wants to happen or what the trouble is, often he or she then knows the right path without you saying anything. As a result, the person feels the satisfaction of solving his or her own problem—and will tell him- or herself what to do next.

If that's all there is to counseling, then what's the big deal? you might ask. Basically, this *is* the process of counseling. But it's not that easy. Sometimes it is difficult to do because people have a hard time knowing where they want to get to, knowing what they want changed, knowing *what* is troubling them. There are many ways to help them, or to hinder them, in giving good advice to themselves. As I review some of these ways, you may find some ideas on how you might answer when someone comes to you with the question of what path to take or what he or she should do about a problem.

What Is the Other Not Saying?

Recently a student came to me asking how he could become involved in assisting in the peer counseling program. Since he was a graduate student, I began our conference by asking him what kind of experience he had had in doing this kind of work. Very quickly, picking up clues from his answer, I was able to uncover the real reason why he had come. He was having problems establishing relationships with women, particularly because of some deep-rooted problems with his mother. I soon realized that he had used a safe, acceptable reason as a means to ask me for help with his problem. He took the chance that I would discover his real need for coming. Have you ever done that when you have needed help? Students often first approach a counselor with a "safe" problem. Sometimes they leave disappointed, because I—or another—wasn't sensitive enough to what the student was *not* saying.

It's so easy to miss the vein of the real problem and work

industriously on a surface one. This might happen when a counselor is nervous—wanting to help but not sure how to proceed. Sometimes the troubled student is anxious, so he or she needs time to talk about safe things before having courage to broach the "risky" problem. The longer the person talks about the surface problem, the more one is convinced it *is* the real one. And sometimes, no matter how much has been said, when the meeting is over you feel as though you've failed.

To give you an example of what I am saying, let's go back to that class that was discussing the decision fantasy. The students had not yet really learned *how* to counsel others. They had only talked about what they should or should not do when they were counseling. Now it was time to practice. David agreed to counsel Pam, who was taking the role of a high school girl. Pam, supposedly overweight and depressed, was meeting with David, a peer counselor, for the first time. A dance was coming up on Friday. This is how David tried to help Pam:

David: How do you feel?

Pam: Oh, OK.

David: Are you going to the dance?

Pam: No, I don't think so . . . I just feel kind of fat, and I never feel like anybody would want to dance with me.

David: Do you want to go with me? I'll take you.

Pam: Would you really? I don't know. I'd feel kind of weird.

David: Why would you feel weird?

Pam: Well, you're popular, and everyone wants to dance with you, but you probably don't know what it's like to just stand around at a dance. You feel like everybody's looking at you.

David: You mean, you're saying, you don't want to go with me to the dance?

Pam: Well, no, I'm not saying that. I guess . . . I mean that would be OK. It's . . .

David: Why would you feel uncomfortable with me? What would everybody be looking at?

Pam: 'Cause that's just what I've experienced before.

David: Don't worry about that; the more you worry, the more it's going to be true. What makes you feel that way?

Pam: Because I've really had people put me down and stuff, say things to me.

David: How does it make you feel?

Pam: Really bad. I may want to either yell something back or go hide someplace.

David: Have you ever asked people why they say that stuff—why they feel that way about you? Maybe they don't even know you.

Pam: I think that's really true . . . they don't know me. But what am I supposed to do—go out and say, "I'm really nice" . . . or

David: Well, that's why I asked you to the dance. I know you and you're nice.

David ended his session with Pam trying to cheer her up—telling her what he thought she wanted to hear. He wanted to help. He was warm and sincere. But did he help her? What happened? What would you have done differently, if you had been David?

This is what I think was going on:

• David needed more information about the problem. He assumed the problems were that Pam was not invited to the dance and that she was fat.
• Even if those *were* the problems, he tried to use quick, easy solutions, such as offering to take Pam to the dance or suggesting she ask people why they were saying negative things about her.
• David turned away from Pam's feelings. Too often we try to help people by telling them *not* to feel. It doesn't work. Instead it hurts! It hurts because you think the other hasn't

listened to your feelings or that they have been rejected. The feelings may not be rational—but you still have them. Even if one can't change how another feels, it does help to show one *recognizes* they are there.

- In pushing his invitation to the dance, David detoured Pam from talking about her depression. Instead, she had to defend her reluctance to accept his offer.

- Basically, David was not asking Pam what she was *not* saying. He could have done this by asking: "What do you mean by people putting you down?" "Who are these people?" "Do you feel you have *any* friends?" "How does your family treat you?" "What do you *like* about yourself?"

People are often afraid to admit what hurts them. But if they are *asked* to talk about what's hurting by someone who is warm and sincere, then sometimes they dare to open up and talk about it. By listening to a stray comment or observing physical behavior, the one who is trying to help might get a clue of what to ask to bring out those feelings. The answers may provide you with the necessary information you need to help.

Asking such questions to get information is not prying or snooping. It's a way of showing you're interested. It is only asking for what is not said. If Pam doesn't want to talk about it she can say: "No, that's not what's bothering me" or, "I don't want to talk about that." Remember, people do know how to defend their privacy. On the other hand, many do not know how to reveal what they want to say, unless they are encouraged by their counselor.

The urgency of this need has been sensitively expressed by an unknown author in a poem called, "Please Hear What I'm Not Saying." In Gilbert Wrenn's condensed and modified version of the poem, you can even more clearly hear the cry to listen, to notice, and to care.

> Don't be fooled by me.
> Don't be fooled by the face I wear,
> For I wear a mask, I wear a thousand masks,

Masks that I am afraid to take off,
But none of them are me.
Pretending is an art that's second nature to me.
But don't be fooled,
For God's sake, don't be fooled.

I give you the impression that I am secure,
That all is sunny and unruffled with me,
Within as well as without,
That confidence is my name and coolness my game,
That the water's calm and I am in command,
And that I need no one.
Don't believe me, Please!

My surface may be smooth,
But my surface is my mask,
My varying and ever-concealing mask.
Beneath lies no smugness,
No complacence.
Beneath dwells the real me,
In confusion and fear,
In loneliness.
I idly chatter with you in the suave tones of surface talk.
I tell you everything that's really nothing,
Of what's crying within me.
So, when I'm going through my routine,
Please don't be fooled by what I'm *not* saying,
And what I'd like to be able to say,
What for *survival* I need to say,
But what I can't say.

Only you can call me into aliveness,
Each time you're kind, and gentle, and encouraging.
Each time you try to understand because you really care,
My heart begins to grow wings,
Very small wings, very feeble wings, but wings.
With your sensitivity and sympathy, and your power of understanding,
You can breathe life into me, I want you to know that.
I want you to know how important you are to me,
How you can be a creator of the person that is me if you choose to.

Please choose to.
Do not pass me by.
It will not be easy for you.
My long conviction of worthlessness builds strong walls.
The nearer you approach to me, the blinder I may strike
 back.
I fight against the very thing I cry out for.
But I am told that love is stronger than strong walls.
In this lies my hope,
My only hope.

Who am I, you may wonder.
I am someone you know very well—
I am a hurting member of your family,
I am the person sitting beside you in this room,
I am every person you meet on the street.
Please don't believe my mask,
Please come behind it to glimpse the real me.
Please speak to me, share a little of yourself with me,
At least *recognize* me.
Please.
Because you care.

If you memorize only the title of this poem, it will remind you of one way to answer when you talk with a friend
about a problem. As you walk down the hall in a crowd or
look around at those in your classroom, think about it. If
you do, you may find you are more sensitive to all those you
meet.

"I Know Just How You Feel!"

John is pouring out his anger, frustration, and dejection to
Kevin as they drive to the Youth Council meeting. It was
caused by another scene with his mother. Every time he goes
somewhere there is an inquisition. She wants to know where,
why, and with whom. "She just doesn't trust me—and I don't
know why! She keeps looking for something that just isn't
there."

Kevin begins listening, but soon is thinking about his own

problems with *his* mother. As John finishes talking, Kevin blurts out, "I know just how you feel!" Then Kevin is off on his own problems.

How do you think John was feeling at about that time? How much help do you think he got from hearing about Kevin's problems? Not much, if any, I would imagine. He didn't for two reasons. First, Kevin said, "I know just how you feel," without finding out if he *did*, in fact, know all of how John felt. Second, he interrupted helping John with his problem by bringing up his own problems.

Do you think Kevin does know *just how John feels?* He may know similar feelings about similar problems. But does that mean he knows what is unique about John's situation? Kevin has done what many of us do in trying to be helpful. Kevin has jumped to a conclusion, perhaps too quickly. In the process, he may have lost an opportunity to help John.

Jumping to conclusions is often the way people respond when asked for help. But it may not be an effective way to help the other know what to do. Milo, the unhappy boy in *The Phantom Tollbooth*, found this out. During his travels he ends up on the Island of Conclusions. When he asks a native how he got there, Canby tells him that every time you decide something without having a good reason, you land on the Island of Conclusions. Milo complains that it is a rather ugly place to be, and Canby agrees. Then he adds, "It does look much better from a distance."

The point, of course, is that things often aren't the way they seem when seen from a distance, without more detailed information. This means that when a problem *seems* similar to one we've had or have, it is important to stop and listen more carefully so we don't miss something important—so we don't miss any facts showing how the other's problem is different from our own. John's background and John's situation may be very different from Kevin's. John's feelings and the reasons for his feelings may be unique to John. A conclusion-jumper may miss John entirely.

What Solutions Have You Considered?

People are seldom empty-handed or empty-headed about what they *might* do to solve their problems. But a person may have mulled over various possibilities so often that he or she now is more confused than ever about what to do. It may be that the last thing needed is yet another solution to consider. Instead, your help may be necessary in reviewing the ones already considered. He or she may insist that your advice is needed but would rather *you* insisted on hearing what thoughts they have already had on the problem.

Actually, you may understand the problem the person faces very accurately. You may think you have a neat suggestion to offer. You're quite sure it would be successful. Even so, hold back on your "gem" of advice until all the person's own ideas have been explored. There are reasons why I urge this:

- Your solution may already have been thought of. If the solution comes from the person's own idea, he or she feels confident when you react positively. If you suggest it first, you lose this opportunity to enhance the other's self-confidence.
- Your solution may be one *you* could carry out, but the other person couldn't—for whatever reason. By freely choosing a solution, the other person is saying that he or she feels both able to do it and willing to try.
- If you suggest what another should do, you are assuming part of the responsibility for what happens if your suggestion is followed. People seldom thank you when a decision turns out well, but they often remember who made the suggestion when the result is negative. Even though the decision is a hard one to make, ultimately individuals prefer to make it themselves and assume their own responsibility for the outcome.

Your help comes in asking your friend questions about the consequences of each alternative he or she is considering. If none of these solutions look promising, *then* offer, tentatively, one you may have. If you too are at a loss for what to suggest, admit it. Then try to think of someone else you both could turn to for more help.

Do You Want to Be Healed?

Healed may be a pretty presumptuous word to use in talking about counseling. However, the word highlights a vivid point I want you to consider when you are helping with a problem. The question is one that Jesus asked of the man at the pool who had wanted to be healed—for years.

You may think it is a stupid question. But the fact is that some people *don't* want to be healed, helped, or free of their problems. They don't because they use their problems to get and keep attention from others. Too often it works! It's hard to ignore someone who says he or she is in trouble.

How can you tell? How can you tell who truly wants help from those who just want to talk about their problems? Well, there are those who are *too* ready to pour out their troubles, who talk freely about them with anyone who will listen. Then there are those who keep repeating their story until you know the details by heart. Often these are friends who resent your questions, deny all your suggestions, and moan about the lack of help they are getting. They may even criticize the help you give.

Everyone has the right to fail—even to keep their problems as pets. We can't help everyone, no matter how much we care. We sincerely must try to help—even to the point, perhaps, of calling attention to what we think the person is doing. But if a friend makes no effort to change his or her situation, then we need to save our energy for others. When we recognize the signs, we can move on freely to another who will in some way answer the question affirmatively— "Yes, I *want* to be healed."

I'VE DONE MY BEST

There will be times when you've tried your hardest to help someone. You've followed all these suggestions. You still feel as though you've failed. Or you may have tried, but for whatever reason, you know you made a mistake. You lost an opportunity to help. David felt this way after trying to help Pam.

At such times this may help: Sometimes we think of counseling or helping as a kind of "performance." If we are nervous, we may forget our "lines," or what we're "supposed" to do. It is almost as though we bring our own invisible audience into the help we are trying to give to another—an audience that looks over our shoulders, listening to catch every slip we make. We can't seem to concentrate on the person who needs the help. We're thinking too much of how *we* are doing.

This happens to me, sometimes, when I know I have a particularly difficult conference. I try to deal with this feeling by telling myself that the purpose of the conference is not to make myself look good. I can only do what at this time is my best. Sometimes this eliminates my invisible audience.

There will be times when you aren't successful. But if your intentions are sincere, the message that you are concerned will come through. It is not your skill or the mechanics you use so much as your loving that matters. When you bring this motivation to the meeting with a friend, you'll be able later to say, "I've done the best I know how at this time. I may do better next time."

GO AND DO AS HE DID

What do I do after I've listened? Much has now been said about what you can do. Perhaps a summary will be helpful, using a model given to us in the story of the Good Samaritan. This man in ancient times was not trying to counsel in the terms we have been using. But in his example he demonstrated the necessary requirements you need to be an effective counselor. Listen to the story as it applies to *you* and your efforts to help.

A certain man on his way from Jerusalem to Jericho was attacked by robbers who stripped him, beat him, and went off leaving him half-dead. Various people passed by, including a priest, and saw him but went on their way without giving aid. However, a Samaritan, an outcast himself, who normally would never associate with this stranger, also came by. Seeing the wounded man, he was moved with compassion. He went to him and bandaged his wounds. He put him on his own beast and took him to an inn and looked after him. The next day he gave the innkeeper money and told him to take care of the wounded man, and if it cost more, he would pay him when he, the Samaritan, returned.

- Of all those who could have helped that day, the Samaritan was the least likely to be expected to help. You may think you are the least likely one to help another. Your problems are even worse, you think. You wouldn't know what to do. Did that stop the Samaritan? He let his heart speak, rather than his head. Your desire may be all you need.
- He bound up his wounds, bathing them with oil and wine. To do this, he had to touch the wounded man, using his own supplies, even endangering himself by exposing himself to possible further attacks by the robbers. You can't help another from a distance and without some risk. You have to investigate the need, touch the inner life of the other, and expose yourself, if you want to help.
- The Samaritan interrupted his own plans and schedule. He also gave his time, energy, and money to assist—the valuable qualities we all find so precious. He gave these to someone he didn't even know. Can a friend ask as much of you?
- He left the inn without receiving any thanks or reward from the man he helped. Maybe the wounded man never knew who helped him. The Samaritan, motivated by a desire to save a life, apparently did not need a reward. Maybe he knew it was enough to have given new life to a fellow travel-

er. His service was given without obligation or expected repayment. This is an example of the highest quality of caring.

Peer counselors often do on a smaller scale what this story describes. Although they aren't perfect, many discover unexpected rewards from attempting to help a peer. Some say they had never before realized the satisfaction one feels in knowing one has had a part in strengthening the life of another. What comes is not a visible reward, but it is a precious one.

You don't have to be a peer counselor for this to happen to you. Much of what peer counselors learn has been explained to you. Be your own teacher. It will help if you remember that many of your peers need a friend, a warm, concerned, even though awkward, friend—and go and do as the Samaritan did.

7

The Me I Am Now and the Person I Am Becoming

I am growing, world.
I am reaching and touching and stretching and testing
And finding new things, new wonderful
Things.
New frightening things.
I'm just growing, world, just now.
I'm not tall, I'm not strong, I'm not
Right.
I'm just trying to be.
I'm a person, I'm me!
Let me test, let me try, let me reach,
Let me fly!
Push me out of my nest (but not too fast).
There is much I don't know.
There are things that I want—don't
Hide me from the sight of the world.
Give me room, give me time. There are things I'm not
    frightened
To try.
Let me tumble and spring, let me go,

Let me be. Wait and see . . .
I am growing, world.
Water me with the wisdom of
Your tears.

—Cherie A. Millard, age 17
(Gisela Konopka, *Young Girls*, p. 14)

Beneath the skin, body shape or build, color of eyes and hair, all that I can see when I look and that I identify with your name, there is a *you*, partially portrayed in Cherie's poem. You are aware of this inner self that you take with you everywhere you go, talking to it daily. You often hid it from yourself. It is that "you" who is reading and touching and stretching and testing and finding new things. It is the voice that asks, "Who am I? Who was I yesterday? Who will I be tomorrow? Who do I want to be when I am finished with tumbling and springing . . . and growing?"

You *are* asking these questions, because you are normal, young—and human. It may be that you've come to the period of your life when searching for answers is necessary. You no longer can be just your mother's son, your brother's sister, or the only child in the family. You have to be a person of your own, one who is unique and separate from others. You want to be pushed out of your nest but not too fast, because there is much you still don't know—about yourself, your future, the world.

The search for answers to your questions involves sorting out your past experiences, thinking about what's happening to you now, and putting together what you find into some kind of picture of your future. Do you know what all this means, what Cherie was really saying in her poem? It means you will be sorting out your values. As you experiment with new experiences, compare yourself to others, observe what others do, listen, and think, you will be seeking the answer to "Who am I?" The answer you will find is that *you are what you value*—now, today, and what you value as you continue shifting, shaping, and molding your life in the days of your tomorrows.

If that is true, then perhaps you can understand why a book about caring should have a chapter devoted just to a discussion of personal values. All the previous chapters involved values, too. But now the *main* topic is the values around which we build our lives and that define our character and the quality of our lives.

Many young people are uncertain about who they are and who they want to be. This means that the peer counseling session devoted to values is a very important part of their training. Students have confessed during this session that they don't know what they value. They aren't even sure they *want* to be a caring person. They are sad, too, that they aren't sure what their friends, or even their parents, value. But they want to be more clear about their own values and beliefs.

So students haltingly begin to talk about who they think they are, the negative feelings they have about themselves, and their doubts about how to handle peer pressure. Eventually they explore their limited understanding of the meaning of integrity, commitment, love, honesty, and even self-esteem. In the beginning sessions of training they were afraid to share this way. They understood what John Powell was saying when he wrote in *Why Am I Afraid to Tell You Who I am?*:

> But, if I tell you who I am, you may not like who I am, and it is all that I have.

Now, trusting one another, they are eager to talk, to learn, and to set goals for the kind of person each wants to become. One of the clear messages they learn is this: Words are cheap expressions of a value. It is only when you back up those words with an expenditure of your time, energy, abilities, and possibly your personal security that you demonstrate that those words actually are part of who you are.

Sorting out values is an interesting process. It is also a sensitive and fragile task. You have to be honest with yourself. Some dislike themselves so much, they can't make themselves explore their inner selves to find what motivates them. It can be painful, but getting in touch with your values is also rewarding. Often, the reason it is difficult is that we don't know how to go about doing it.

If you're not frightened by the prospect of exploring yourself, I'd like to help you do it. It will mean going on an armchair journey, stopping at points to take a look at what was seen or learned along the way. When we end, you may have a clearer picture of who you are and perhaps a sketch of who you want to become. When you take this journey, you may find it triggers emotions that disturb you. If you feel yourself getting a little overwhelmed by these emotions, take a break. Call a friend. Go for a swim or a game of tennis. Do something to shift your thinking for a time. Then go back and continue the journey. If you feel you are ready, let's be off!

THE JOURNEY

It will be easier for you to take this journey if you can get someone to read the "map" to you while you sit with your eyes closed. Have it read slowly, pausing, when asked to, long enough to collect all your thoughts after each interval. If you do it yourself, read a paragraph, which I call an "interval." Next, close your eyes and rummage through your thoughts. Then go on to the next "interval." Find a place where you are comfortable and where you won't be disturbed. If your train of thought is broken, you might lose some of the more important thoughts that have come to you.

First Lap: The Past

Interval 1

Close your eyes and think back to your first memories as a child, up to the time when you finished the sixth grade. First, think about the house or houses you lived in during this period. Choose one of the houses, and in your memory, walk into the house. Now *slowly* walk from room to room, stopping to look around in each. Notice what furniture is there; what colors are in the room; the location of the windows; what is on the walls. Smell any smells that come to mind. Listen to the noise of the silence of each room. Remember how each room made you feel. Do this now, and when you have finished, we'll pause for a moment. (Pause.)

Interval 2

Now I want you to go to your favorite room in this house, or the place you enjoyed the most. If it is the TV room, turn it off; if it is your bedroom, close the door. Imagine yourself sitting here comfortably. Now look at yourself. What are you wearing? Are these your favorite clothes? How old are you? What do you like to do in this room? What is your favorite possession? Is it a dog, cat, book, record, toy, teddy bear, game? What do you like to eat? Think about yourself as you sit quietly and comfortably in this room. (Pause.)

Interval 3

Keep on thinking about yourself. Do you think of yourself as small, or big; quiet, or loud; sunny, or sad; attractive, or ugly? Do you like your body? If so, why? What don't you like about it? Do you like yourself at this place in your life? Do you think others like you? Why, or why not? Is it hard to think about yourself at this age? What other thoughts come to you as you sit thinking about yourself? (Pause.)

Interval 4

Now think about the people in this house. Who lives with you? Is there your father? Your mother? Possibly your grandmother? What about brothers and sisters? Of all these people, to whom do you feel closest? Which ones do you fight with most? Who loves you most? Whom do you admire? Who is it important to please? How do you feel about yourself when you are with each of these people? What makes it hard or easy to live with them? (Pause.)

Interval 5

Now, in your memory, begin walking or riding to school. What are your feelings as you think of school? What do you look forward to? What do you dread? Which teacher do you think of first? What class or subject do you remember most? What do you feel as you sit in your favorite class? Who were your best friends at this time in your life? Whom did you dislike, and why? What role did you have at school?—clown? serious student? best student? Were you made fun of? What nicknames did you have? Were these pleasing to you, or distasteful? (Pause.)

Interval 6

Now let's go through a typical day as you remember it. What were your activities? How about sports? Were you in the Christmas play or a piano recital? What did you do during lunch? What about after school? Were you leaving school happy or sad? What was the best thing that happened at this point in your life? Why was it good? What was the worst or most painful event of that period of school life? Why was it painful? (Pause.)

Interval 7

Let's leave school behind and think about weekends and vacations. What were your weekends like? Did you sleep late, help around the house or yard? Did you watch TV? How much time did you spend alone? Did you go to church or temple? What things did you do with your family? How about summers? Were they long and boring, or full and exciting? What was the best trip you took on a vacation? Did you have a job? What smells or pictures come into your mind when you think of summers at this period of your life? (Pause.)

This is the end of the first lap of your journey.

Did you enjoy it, or was it painful? You were asked to think about a lot of things. What memories did this release? After you think awhile, take out a piece of paper and write answers to some of the following questions:

1. **What was missing from that period of your life?**

2. What three things, conditions, or experiences are your most vivid memories?
3. What feelings did you have about yourself then that you still have?
4. What different feelings do you *now* have about yourself?
5. If you could live this period again, what would you do differently?
6. What other impressions or reactions did this journey bring out?

I told you earlier that exploring one's values would not be easy. But can you see some meaning or purpose in doing it? It may not have been easy for you to answer the questions about that period of your life—or even to think about it. But please try. If it is hard, ask yourself why. What emotions do these memories stir up? What might you want to avoid or forget in thinking about the past? After you've thought about this and tried again to answer the questions, we'll go on to the second lap of the trip.

Second Lap: The Present

Interval 1

Now let's explore your life as it is now. In your thoughts, go to the house where you live now. It may not be the same house as the one of your past. Think about how you feel *now* in this house. Mentally move from room to room, gathering feelings when you are in each room. What causes these feelings? Now think about going to the room you call your own. Think about the things that belong to you in this room—your clothes, the things in your drawers, the objects on the walls, the colors in the room. What do these things say to you? If a stranger walked in, without knowing you what might he or she learn about you as the person to whom this room belongs? Think about this. (Pause.)

Interval 2

Now, mentally go to school, if you are still in school. Who are the important people to you in this school? Who is your favorite teacher? Who are your friends? What do you like about them? What do you have in common? Are you well known around school? If so, why? What has meaning for you in this school? Is it getting good grades? earning a diploma? having fun? being in leadership positions? participating in sports? knowing your teachers or professors? being involved in service activities? Do you like yourself when you are at school? Are you comfortable there? Would you rather be someplace else? (Pause.)

If you are not in school, mentally go the place where you work—or your home, if you are a full-time homemaker. Who are the important people to you at your job? Who do you like and respect among your associates or supervisors? Why do you respect them? What do you have in common? Are you well known at your job or throughout your profession? If so, why? What has meaning for you in your work? Is it the kind of work you do? the salary you make? the chances to travel or take people out to lunch? opportunities for promotions and advancement? freedom to make your own schedule, plan your own day? involvement in important decisions? the activities it provides? Do you like yourself when you are at work? Are you comfortable there? Would you rather be someplace else, either not working or doing a different kind of work? (Pause.)

Interval 3

How about your evenings, weekends, and vacations? What are they like? What responsibilities do you have? Do you belong to clubs or organizations? What do you do for fun? What turns you on? Is it soccer or backpacking, golf or gardening? Cruising around with friends or polishing your car? dating? sitting and looking at the stars? writing poetry? watching TV? going on a retreat with your church group. going camping? listening to music? being with a friend and talking? lying on your back and thinking? What *does* make you feel good and make your life seem worthwhile? (Pause.)

Interval 4

Finally, come back to yourself—in utter privacy, honestly, frankly, and flat-out. No one will know what you are thinking. What kind of a person do you think you are? What do you like about yourself? What don't you like? Are you physically attractive? Why, or why not? What kinds of people are attracted to you? If you were a stranger and were to meet yourself for the first time, would you like yourself? What things do you want to hide from others? What do you want people to know about you? Do you feel useful? Are you contributing to others? What makes you feel good about yourself, or bad? What else do you think about when you think about yourself? (Pause.)

This is the end of the second lap of the journey.

Was this more difficult to do than the first lap? Was it harder to look at yourself as you are now, or was it harder when you reviewed the past? What intervals seemed the hardest? When you've given this some thought, answer the following questions. Take out your paper again and see what you can answer about the following:

1. What do you seek in your life that you don't now have?
2. What is important in your life that you want to keep?
3. What qualities would you most want others to find in you?
4. What parts of your life, or yourself, would you like to change?
5. What other reactions did you have when you thought about your present life?
6. If you couldn't or didn't think through any of the intervals, why?

Third Lap: The Future

Interval 1

Now we move to your imagination rather than your memory. Imagine walking down a corridor leading to a room called the future. You go through many twists and turns and walk by numerous passages leading off to different "futures." You sometimes are not sure what direction to take. As you see yourself walking, searching, are you walking fast, eagerly and expectantly wanting to know what you'll find in that room of the future? Or are you strolling in a leisurely manner, occasionally looking back at what you've left?

On your back you're carrying a backpack holding the things you want to bring with you into the future, including your dreams and desires. Feel it on your back. Does it feel heavy, or light? Is the pack jammed full, or almost empty? What memories are stored in that pack that you don't want to lose? Any achievements? What dreams or desires? Are there desires for power and position? for specific achievements? for closer relationships with people? Or is the dream compartment empty because you haven't thought about what you want in the future? Maybe you haven't because you either dread the future or doubt you could ever get what you want. What *are* your feelings as you walk along? Do you feel lonely? anxious? excited? confident? sad? happy? confused? Do you feel exposed and vulnerable, or protected and secure? Try to make yourself get in touch with the feelings you have when you think about the future. (Pause.)

Interval 2

Image you have arrived at the door of the future. Slowly open the door and look in. What is your first impression as you gaze at the room? Is it bathed in sunshine and light, or is it dark and gloomy? Is it a huge, spacious room, or small and cavelike? Do you want to go in and explore, or do you feel afraid to move over the threshold? (Pause.)

Interval 3

Now think about walking into the room and looking around to see what is going on and who is there. Are people studying, working, playing, or standing around talking? Do you want to join them? If so, what do you want to do the most of? Where do you want to spend your time? What do you visualize yourself doing in that room of the future? Or do you just see yourself sitting, watching others? Think about this. (Pause.)

Interval 4

Finally, look around the room and think about what you feel you would need to have there for you to be satisfied to spend the rest of your life in that room. Would it be certain people: certain activities? Is it specific work to be accomplished? What material things must be there? What chances for pleasure? What is needed to let you live in that room with no regrets? After thinking about this for a moment, seriously and honestly turn and look at yourself. Go beyond your outer appearance as you think you will look in the future and study that inner self. What is it doing, thinking, feeling? Will it still be reaching, touching, stretching, and testing in that room of the future? What do you hope will be changed about that inner self? What have you added to that self by learning, experience, pain, effort, perhaps some sacrifice and work: Is there anything in that room of the future that could still help you mold that self to what you want it to be? What still needs to be done so you can approach the door to leave, walking proudly and contented. Spend some time thinking about this as we end our arm-chair journey. (Pause.)

Was it hard, or even impossible, to go through the future lap of the journey? It is for most people. It is because it asks you to explore deep inside yourself and examine what holds your life together and keeps you going. Such a look into the future requires you to be honest about your beliefs about yourself, and to admit the commitments and decisions that are now shaping your life. It's also difficult to think of a future because there are many unknowns and unpredictable events in that future. But the reality of life is that we may, on the one hand, drift into the future or allow ourselves to be pushed into it by others. We may, on the other hand, chart our own course and attempt to move steadily in the direction of what we want that future to be.

Wait a bit before you write down any thoughts that you may have collected on this lap of your journey. The rest of our discussion on values may help you think more clearly about that future.

THE VALUE OF LIFE ITSELF

Your room of the future, whether it is tomorrow, next week, a year, or ten years from now, will be constructed out of the value you put on life itself. What is life for? What is the value of *your* life? What is a good life to you? What does life happiness and satisfaction mean to you?

It is an awesome thought that each of us is completely unique. Among all of the seventy billion people that have ever lived upon this earth there is no one just like you. You are a rarity, a unique creation, an original that can't be copied. The earth has never seen, nor ever will see, someone just like you. You deserve to respect yourself as a creation so precious that you should want to develop all that has been given to you.

Each of us was given certain talents and abilities, some of them found only in us. These are to be developed and used to help and serve both ourselves and others. Or they can be used for self alone, or not at all. Every time you deny those talents and your own uniqueness, or say you can't do something before you've tried, you're closing off some part of that room of the future. Each time you put yourself down by comparing yourself unfavorably with others, you're copping out of life.

It is sad that many young people today do not believe their lives are valuable, that their lives have meaning. Some are confused about the purpose of life. Some believe their lives are their own to waste in any way that they please.

What do *you* believe? Before you answer, listen to what John Powell has to say:

> So you and I must look into ourselves at the deepest level, the point at which few people, if any, are ever permitted to know us. What do we *really* want from life? What do we *really* think would make us happy? You and I are now practicing a life principle, which may not be obvious from a surface view. Someday it will amount to a life wager. In the end everyone gambles his or her life on something, or someone, as the way to happiness. (*Unconditional Love*, p. 34)

THE GAMBLES OF FINDING HAPPINESS

As I sit and talk with many young people, listening to what they say, observing what they do, I hear and see patterns to their search for meaning and happiness in life. These patterns are evident in the "methods" they use to handle their daily existence. These methods are the gambles they take to get out of life what they want. Such gambles are representative of the different passageways open to you as you go down the corridor to your future. These patterns become the life wager that Powell talks about, some of which lead to a future that is bankrupt and empty, some to a future that is rich and full—and happy. Let's talk about some of these "gambles." As we do, see if any apply to you, and whether or not you may agree with me about the risk you take when you gamble.

1. The Gamble of Full-time Pleasure

This life pattern is one of having fun and seeking pleasure from one exciting experience after another. Those who live this gamble often try anything—the more risky it is, the more exciting for them. There is little discrimination in the activities in which they become involved. They seldom go into any activity or interest in any depth. Rather, they look always for something "new." Diversion is the name of the game called fun. When diverted, their minds don't have to think about what they don't like to think about, themselves or their lives. What's wrong with this, you ask? What do you stand to lose? Again, I want to let John Powell provide an answer:

> Becoming a person, therefore, involves the sacrifice of some experiences in order to experience more deeply the values which are connected with and which promote one's own destiny. Having decided what we want to be and want to do, we must exercise some selection in the experiences we seek, choosing those which are conducive to our goals and refusing those which could only detour us. (*Unconditional Love*, p. 509)

Having fun and pleasure in life is desirable and good. But little real pleasure comes from seeking it directly. Rather, it is often the by-product of seeking other goals and commitments.

2. The Gamble of "It's Gotta Be Me"

During your lifetime you have been living in a society that has promoted "doing your own thing" as the means to finding life satisfaction. Do you believe it? Is this your philosophy of life? This philosophy is self-centered; it says no to the needs of others and to your need of them. It creates isolation and creates a fierce competitiveness with those around you. Everything you do is motivated by the question, What will I get out of this for myself? The result is, you don't get much. You sacrifice the benefits of sharing; of knowing the security of trusting and being trusted; of being able to fail without it being a catastrophe; of admiring another who does well; of doing something for another without an expected return.

3. The Gamble of Escape

This pattern is one of running when things get tough or when one feels uncomfortable. Examples of its use range from getting out of a difficult class or dropping a friend who doesn't fit in to avoiding talking through a problem with someone you care about. In the end, it can mean running away from home or moving out if you can't get along. It is a way of life that avoids the possibility of failure by not attempting anything that is hard or by not getting involved for fear you might be hurt or there might be work involved. It eventually leads to no feelings or commitments, to *observing* life, rather than living it. As one student said when asked to name a person who had helped him in his life, "I have never needed anyone. I have done it by myself. I tend to avoid situations where I may need someone." When pushed to say what he would do if he, in fact, found he *did* need someone, he finally said, "I don't want to think about that. I hope it never happens."

4. The Gamble of Balancing the Account

This is the win/lose approach to life, or living by the rule "If I do this for you, then you'll do this for me." The other part of the agreement, though, is "I'll get even with you for what you did or didn't do." This approach can mean revenge. If a person lives this way he or she must always keep an account of what has been done and whether it has been paid back. "Since my mother did this to me, I'm going to do this back." "If I say I'm sorry, won't he think he's won?" If you're going through life making sure the accounts are balanced, you won't have much time to develop your own life and future. You will also be only responding or reacting to what others have done—done to, or for, you. This doesn't sound like a satisfying way to live.

5. The Gamble of Using Your Life as the Price of Admission

It is sad to see how many young people devalue themselves by what they say and do to be accepted or get something they think they want. Often young people begin misusing their bodies by smoking or using alcohol and other drugs to be part of the gang. Mike's father asked him what he would do if a good friend wanted Mike to smoke a joint with him, and he didn't want to. Mike, who was an eighth grader, was slow to answer. Then he finally said, "I don't know *what* I would do, Dad. It is really tough, especially if you like your friend." Mike is afraid he will lose a friend if he listens to his own desires and refuses the joint. But how will he feel about himself if he gives in? Will he be giving up a part of himself? Some girls may use their bodies to be noticed and get recognition, often in negative ways. But are they respected? Some young people get into heavy and sometimes harmful sexual relationships hoping to keep a boy friend or girl friend, or to feel loved by someone.

When you find you are going against your own desires, using or misusing your body to be accepted, or can't say no to peer pressures, you are "giving yourself away" bit by bit. Others are using you selfishly. You are, in fact, saying that you don't value yourself, and it then follows, why should others value you either? It's a high price to pay. It can become the life wager that leaves you empty and unfulfilled.

THE GAMBLES OF COMMITMENTS

There are alternatives—alternatives that require sacrifice and hard work, even pain and disappointment. But these may also be the ones that produce the satisfactions that people long for in life. These are the commitments students discuss, learn about, and gradually begin to try in peer counseling. The two I'll explain are not totally different from one another, but each has a different theme.

1. The Commitment to Risk Your Life for a Useful Purpose

How about approaching your life with the commitment that the world will be a better place because you've lived in it? With your talents and abilities, refined through education, training, and experience, you commit yourself to do something to benefit your country, town, neighborhood, or perhaps your family. This can be done through a vocation, a job, or family life; sometimes it is through volunteer work or hobbies. It could mean that you tackle a big "job," or a small, unnoticed activity that seems to be routine.

This commitment requires observing what needs to be done—listening to how people hurt, caring about the quality and conditions of the lives of others. It also means you have to acknowledge your talents and decide how they can be used. You will need discipline, planning, and perhaps giving up of free time to do this. But you will get some rewards.

People we admire throughout history have been those who were willing to risk security and safety, to give up immediate pleasure so that others might have healthier, freer, more culturally enriched lives. They did not confuse a good life with having a good time. They were willing to take a stand for what they believed. They didn't reject the idea that one person could make a difference. It is to be hoped that there are a number of people like this around today.

I know plenty of young people who have a commitment to a life goal or purpose. They are different from their peers because they aren't bored or always looking for "something to do." They get up in the morning ready to go. They have energy and their faces are alive with expression. They don't care if they are classified as "different," or if they suffer some sneers when they stick up for another or for something they value. Working toward their goals, they sense they are becoming more the person they have decided they want to be. If you haven't made this kind of decision, or decided on some purpose for *your* life, what are your alternatives? Where or to what do these alternatives lead? Think about this.

2. The Commitment to Risk Care and Love for Others

Francis of Assisi said, "It is in giving that we receive." This is the message of the commitment to risk care and love for others—and is the whole theme of this book. It sounds so simple, but it is hard to put into practice. Your head may agree, but your heart has to produce the results.

A lack of love is why so many people have meaningless and unfulfilled lives. I propose that *you* can't have a meaningful life without the experience of love, without the commitment of yourself to another or to others. This famine of love has been created largely by the "I-am-number-one-and-you-don't-count" philosophy mentioned earlier. It also partially explains the attraction of cults, because they offer the illusion of friendship, love, and respect, supposedly with no strings attached—until later.

Love as an emotion, nourishment, or life force can only be lost by not giving it to others or by refusing to let oneself feel it. Much love wants in return a recognition of the love that is given. This is selfish, but it is also very human. Many people know only this kind of love. Many do not know there is also a love of which we are capable that has no conditions—a love that expects nothing in return. When you can achieve an ability to love unconditionally, you can then put another's needs and desires ahead of yours; you can let another win; you can forgive; and you can value the inner person despite what the outer person says or does.

Viktor Frankl once said, "True self-esteem and a true sense of identity can be found only in the reflected [thoughtful] appraisal of those whom we have loved." You risk when you love others. But if it is genuine, you will learn what love can be and do and will discover what power it has to bring you to genuinely loving yourself. Someone else put it this way: Sometimes our light goes out, but is blown again into flame by an encounter with another human being. Each of us owes the deepest thanks to those who rekindle this inner light.

THE PRICE OF YOUR LIFE

There is quite a difference between existing and living. I must be careful in my choice of values, of what I seek in life. I had better not drop the pebbles of my life into the stream of life to go I know not where. We *exist* by breathing, eating, and sleeping. We *live* by using our talents, working on goals, trusting another, sharing, knowing failures, exposing ourselves to being hurt, and entering into relationships.

As we move through each day, week, year, of our lives, we make a staggering number of decisions. How we decide gradually shapes us into a certain kind of person, with a particular kind of character. The alternatives, or paths, we choose ultimately determine the design of what our future will be. When a day is gone, it can't be reclaimed; when a year has passed, it can't be lived again. The days and years of our lives can be allowed to slip away casually, or they can be hoarded selfishly, turning life into an empty shell. The alternative is to build a life that is actively *lived*, not endured.

Earlier I said you *are* what you value—what you really want from life and what you seek to make you happy. I cannot tell you what you *should* value. The heart has no doorknob on the outside that can be opened by another. Only you can open from within. What you let in, bring in, remove, and maintain determines who you are and the kind of person you want to be. When you go through the exit door of the future, who will you be? What will you have gained? *You* must decide.

DECIDING AND BECOMING

All that we've covered about life patterns, principles, and wagers is pretty "heavy" stuff, not absorbed very quickly. Why not go back and reread "The Future" lap of the journey and what follows. Take some time to think. Then write down your thoughts about you and *your* future. You will find at the end of the chapter a list of traits and qualities you might desire to reach for as you grow into the person you are becoming. Rank these according to their importance to you. Then think about how you might acquire them. Here are some questions to get you started:

- How would you like to see yourself be different as an adult from how you see yourself now?
- What would turn your life into "living" rather than existing?
- What life standards would you like to live by in your future?
- What is the most important thing about yourself that you want to change, or that you want to see grow and develop?

WHO PEER COUNSELORS BECOME

It is easy to talk about the kind of person you want to be, a little harder actually to think about it, and an engrossing task over the years to fully become that person. Peer counselors talk a lot about the kind of persons they want to be. Many students, on entering the program, find that to handle their lives they are using the "gamble" methods described earlier. Some don't like themselves, and some have never heard of unconditional love. During the training, many begin to consider the alternative of making such commitments as taking the risk to care, love, and be useful to others. While learning the skills of caring, gradually they are educating their hears to want to care, even when their minds still tell them it is impossible to become that kind of a person.

However, some begin to practice—trying to be more caring of a classmate or kinder to a new student or trying to offer help to someone who needs it. Then they see the results of their efforts. Someone changes his or her behavior; a quiet, depressed classmate seems happier and more alive; one's own family becomes closer and warmer. Finally, they become aware of how they are changing. They like themselves more. New things are important to them; some old things don't seem to matter. Spontaneously they are being more kind and helpful to members of their families and to classmates. Their faces light up with the discovery of what personal satisfaction means. They feel rewarded by something far more precious than class credits or earned money.

Many peer counselors eventually do a lot of thinking about what they want to do with their lives. Some investigate careers in which they can continue working directly with people in helping ways. Katie, for example, plans on becoming a drug counselor to teenaged students. When she was fifteen, she had an abortion. She was an alcoholic at sixteen. Following treatment for her alcoholism and personal problems, she entered a peer counseling training class at age eighteen and decided to prepare herself to become a counselor.

Many peer counselors experience their own lives being rekindled by encountering a human being for whom they have rekindled self-respect and a sense of worth. Through the program, young people are helped to become the person each wants to be. It works both ways. Those who have learned to care for others find out who *they* want to become in the process of helping another.

PERSONAL TRAITS OR QUALITIES CHECKLIST

Here is a list of traits and qualities a person might want to have. Check the ones that seem important to *you*. Then rank ten of them, starting with 1 as the *most* important. Try to be honest with yourself. Forget what you think others might think is important.

_____ Being liked by many friends and being socially active.

_____ Being well liked by a few friends.

_____ Being independent in thought and action.

_____ Having specific interests that you explore deeply.

_____ Having opinions and ideas that you are able to express.

_____ Becoming self-disciplined.

_____ Being able to be alone for regular periods of time.

_____ Being able to stand up under group pressure, doing what you personally desire and value.

137

_____ Appreciating and enjoying yourself as a man or woman.

_____ Finding yourself maturing by regular spiritual devotions or meditations.

_____ Being able to share with another.

_____ Being able to trust another.

_____ Being able to depend on another.

_____ Being able to establish a strong, loving, enduring family.

_____ Being able to forgive another who has hurt you.

_____ Being able to let go of angry or revengeful feelings toward another person, group, or event.

_____ Being able to show care to another unselfishly.

_____ Being able to be a positive, enthusiastic person without being phony.

_____ Being able to accept your own limitations without condemning or disliking yourself.

_____ Being able to give up today's pleasure and diversions for something you want more.

_____ Being able to decide on some goal or purpose for your life.

_____ Being able to make decisions morally.

_____ Being able to be honest with yourself and others.

_____ Being able to accept failures and learn from them.

8

//////////

It's Hard to
Say Good-bye

It happened on a bright, sunny Saturday morning, one July. We were busy unpacking the moving boxes and putting our new house in order. Later that day, I was planning to make apricot jam before preparing for company coming for dinner. Then the phone rang. It was Mother calling from Seattle. Dad had just died of a heart attack. He was gone, dying suddenly and quietly. As I tried to comprehend the finality of her words, my lips could only say, "Now he won't get to see our new house." Only a week before he had called asking when he and Mother could come down to see it.

My dad's death was my first experience of a personal grief that rocked the flow of my life. He had been a sturdy prop in my life, having fed my growth and development with love, wisdom, and humor. I admired and respected him. I wanted to become the kind of person he was. When he died, I began to learn about death—its shock, its physical finality. I also learned about loss and grief, about the healing comfort of my spiritual faith and what human comfort can do to make it easier. *And,* I learned about living—about what is important; what values I want to express in order to have his quality of life; how each day can be used to build a life with meaning as he had known it. I found he was still part of my life through memories. In death, he gave me gifts that have continued to strengthen my life.

It may seem a bit abrupt to shift from all that has been said about living in the previous chapters to thinking of death and saying good-bye. But dying is part of living. As Dr. Michael Scala has said, "The contemplation of death is a very creative exercise. Death provides an essential frame for our lives and gives value to our relationships and endeavors; it forces us to 'get with it' and stop denying or procrastinating. Death is not only natural and inevitable, but necessary. We *need* to die." Elisabeth Kübler-Ross, who has taught us so much about death and dying, also expresses this creative, living view of death: "If you can begin to see death as an invisible, but friendly companion on your life's journey— gently reminding you not to wait until tomorrow to do what you mean to do—then you can learn to *live* your life rather than simply passing through it" (*Death: The Final Stage of Growth*, p. x).

What have been *your* experiences with death? If you have lost a loved one, or even a pet, to death, have you talked about this with anyone? Have you heard your parents discuss death? Probably not many of you can answer yes to these questions. If you can, I wonder if you have talked about what death means to you, what you believe happens after death, or what it will be like to die. I wonder about these things because often the subject of death is avoided. It's all right to talk about it as an *academic* topic, but there are few opportunities to discuss how to handle death when it affects someone you love or your thoughts and possible fears about the fact that some day you, too, will die. We shy away from discussions of this kind. Yet Dr. Robert Wrenn has found in teaching college freshmen and sophomores that the subject of death has always been one of the best vehicles for stimulating class discussion—even better, some semesters, than discussions about sex.

Several years ago, Jim, as a seventh grader, was in peer counseling training. He had just learned about how to welcome a stranger and, seeing a boy sitting alone in the cafeteria, decided to try it. After getting into a lively conversation with the boy, and enjoying it, he asked his "stranger" what he would be doing during summer vacation, starting in two weeks. The boy answered "I'm not sure I'll be around then." Confused by his comment, Jim asked what he meant. The boy said without hesitation, "I have leukemia and my doctor doesn't know if I will live that long." Totally unhinged, not knowing what to say, Jim fled the scene without another word. The next week at his training session, he blurted out his story, still agitated and upset. Then he looked at the leader and the group and asked, "What *do* you say to someone who is dying?"

Yes, Jim, what *do* you say? To help answer that question, a session on death and dying was added to the training. It *is* a hard one. Often there are tears, sometimes anger, and frequently some confusion and awkwardness. Students unfamiliar with death are just as involved by listening as those who are talking about their experiences. For many, this is their first opportunity to talk and learn about death, and it is important to them.

Sometimes the discussions turn to the similarities of physical death and the loss of a friendship. Most young people know what it is like to lose a friend—by moving, an argument, or a change in lifestyle or interests. Sometimes talking about the "good-byes" of friendship helps to get in touch with a better understanding of physical death.

Learning how to be comfortable with the reality of death is another lesson in how to become a caring person. This is why this chapter is important. As I lead you through thinking about death, your feelings about it and what it means to you as well as the experiences you have had with it, you'll begin to see why it is hard to say good-bye. Then we'll consider what each of you can do to help others who are having to say good-bye. Sometimes our caring falters when caring means comforting a grieving friend. We never know when we will encounter our invisible life companion, death. But when we do, we need to know how to say good-bye and how to help others do the same.

TURNING THE PAGE TO A NEW CHAPTER

An elderly friend of mine died after a year's battle with cancer. Although she wasn't severely ill during her last year, she must have felt the end was near. A few weeks before she died, she wrote a letter to those she was leaving behind. It was read at her memorial service. It was as though Alma was present, speaking to each of us sitting in that church. She asked us not to weep for her, or for ourselves. We were to remember the happy times together and the good things life had given her. She said her life had been full; she did not fear death; she was only closing one chapter of life and turning the page to the next one which she eagerly was beginning.

I *did* cry, because of the feelings of hope and comfort her words gave me. They reminded me of my life and what I still wanted to do to fulfill it, what I wanted to do before I was ready to turn the page to the chapter she was beginning. Most young people are eagerly awaiting turning the page to the chapter of life called being "grown up"—the chapter of the opportunities and adventures of adult life. So death may seem far away and remote. Stop, though, and think. Try to get in touch with *your* feelings about death. What fears do you recognize? What thoughts go through your head? What questions do you have? What answers have you found?

Because this is important, I am again going to ask you to close your eyes and let your thoughts wander. After reading what I suggest you think about, close your eyes and see what comes. There aren't any "right" thoughts or feelings in doing this—only a way of leading you into something that is often hard for people to do: thinking about death.

When you're ready, start by noting the first thoughts and feelings that come to you when you think about death. What happens at death? What do you think happens after death? Is there life after death? If so, what's it like? How do you feel about what you leave behind? Do you often, seldom, or never, think about death? Why? (Now, think a moment.)

Now think about the people you love and care about. What would happen to you if any of these people should die? How would their deaths affect you? How might this change your life or how you feel about life or about those still living? Who would you go to for comfort? What spiritual or emotional resources do you have that would help you at this time? (Now, think a moment.)

Now think about yourself. How long do you think you will live? Can you see yourself getting old? If you had the choice, how would you prefer to die? What preparations do you want to have made for your death? (Now, think a moment.)

Finally, think about your experiences with death. If there are none, think about something else you've lost, such as a pet or a friendship. What did these losses mean to you? What was the most painful part of these experiences? What, or who, helped you at that time? What regrets or memories do you have? Was there anything positive that resulted from these losses? (Spend a little more time thinking about all of this.)

THE EXPERIENCES OF DEATH

As I sit doing my thinking about death, I am looking out at a gnarled old oak tree. At the base of the tree is a hole,

145

repaired from its rotting and now cemented over. Carved in the cement is the year 1979. Big, unique Nick was the doctor of the tree, lovingly caring for it as part of the property he used to tend when it was still apple orchards and strawberry patches. When he was almost finished with his "doctoring," he put in the date. When this was done, we visited for a while while he sat in his battered pick-up. We talked about all the beauty of nature, the condition of society, how good life had been—and strangely enough—about death. A month later he died. Now, as I walk along the paths he laid for us and look at the wood he cut for fires, he still seems alive in my life. Often, when driving past the gas station, I look to see if I can't see the pick-up turning in or rumbling down the lane to his house. The only time I ever saw him in a suit and tie was when he lay in his casket. As I looked then, I said my last good-bye—and thanks.

Students, both youth and adults, have shared such memories in peer counseling sessions on death and dying. That's why I had you spend time thinking about your experiences with death. As people talk, cry, share—and comfort—all of us grow, learn, and find strength. Some find relief from a burden they have been carrying emotionally; some decide to change a relationship; some quit postponing something they have wanted to do; many take a different look at their lives. Listen to what some have said.

"I hated my father. I always fought with him. Then one night we had a big argument and I left in anger and went off to a party. The next morning he was dead. At first I couldn't cry. Then awful feelings came over me. At school my friends who knew about my bad feelings about Dad said things like, 'I'll bet you're glad.' That really hurt. I had so much I needed and wanted to say to him. Now it's too late."

"She called and wanted to see me. I told her I was busy . . . that I needed to do something that night. Then the next morning she was dead. She killed herself soon after she hung up from calling me."

***

"My father was a tyrant . . . even during the long period of his last illness. When he died, I was relieved . . . and then I felt guilty. I was sad. I couldn't change our relationship while he lived. He wasn't a happy man, but now he doesn't have to be unhappy any more. Now I'm unhappy and it gets worse each year."

***

"My son was bright and young. He was leaving to go to college. Then he died. He died of a combination of alcohol and pills . . . the kind of thing he had seen me using for so long. He thought they were safe. They called it a suicide. But I was the one who killed him. I'm the one responsible. I live with it daily."

***

"My sister died when she was only a few months old. She had a congenital disease. I suppose it's good that she died, but it seems so unfair. Why should a child who hasn't had a chance to try out life have it taken away?"

***

"My uncle and aunt died. Then a month later, another aunt died. Then my grandfather died. It was my grandfather that hurt the most because I knew he really loved me. My father has never talked to me about it. I wasn't allowed to go to the funeral. I've never gotten to say good-bye."

Amid all the painful stories pouring out of hurting hearts, there is a message about living. There are no human alternatives to death. No replays or revisions are allowed us so that we can correct a relationship or do something differently. The finality of death, its irrevocable good-bye, does shock life into a clearer focus of what's really important about living. Death leaves you with the reminder of days and years you do have left to build your life around that new perspective of what is important and lasting. This can lead you to a better use of your life and greater care of the relationships you now still have. When the grieving person accepts this possibility, then the crying heart and the troubled mind begin to heal.

What could or would you say to each of these hurting people if they came to you with their stories? How could you aid each to gather him- or herself together and to continue on with life? How could you comfort *yourself* if you were one of these people? Your thoughts about death and your understanding of the pain and regrets associated with it will affect what you say or do. So let's talk about some answers to these questions and what you could do to help a grieving friend.

WHY IT'S SO HARD TO SAY GOOD-BYE

Good-bye can be said lightheartedly, as you wave to someone leaving; the return, "See you later," is reassuring. Sometimes you say good-bye with sadness, knowing it will be a long time before you see the other again. The "see-you-soons" just won't happen. Then there is the good-bye that means forever. The voice, the smile, the hug, the touch of the hand are no longer. You no longer have the physical companionship of the one who died. Surely these good-byes are the toughest. It's *obvious* why it is hard to say them. But why is it harder for some than for others? What causes the deep pain when we're forced to say that last farewell? There are different kinds of grief, caused by different circumstances or types of pain. Knowing this, and being able to recognize the differences, can help to guide you in what you do for others and in the kind of comfort you offer.

You heard some of the sources of pain in the comments about people's experiences with death. But there are other sources, too. To help you understand the different causes of grief, I'm going to discuss in some detail five that I often hear. Then we'll go into specifics of what you can do to help, depending on the individual need of the grieving friend.

Your Emotional Well-being Is Fractured

When someone you love dies, part of you goes with him or her. Your emotional security is rocked. Intense feelings of loss fill you as you realize this person is no longer going to be around. You can't turn to him or her for human companionship, happiness, support. This same feeling of loss can come in losing a pet who is close to you. Marsha said her cat had been her comfort when she was low; a companion to play with. The cat had been sensitive to her moods and seemed to understand what to do. Although he had been dead a year, she still missed him and looked for him when she came home. Her cat's death had been an emotional fracture in her life.

Even now, years later, I cry when I hear certain music that reminds me of my father or smell the aroma of a wood campfire or have a problem and need his wisdom. Many happy things are frequent reminders of the person we miss. But memories also keep the person living inside us. At first these memories are painful. But eventually they are comforting, because they are the enduring part of the person you love.

You may not yet know this, if you have not had death enter your life. If not, consider what it might be like to lose someone important to you now. What would happen to your world if he or she died? The feelings that emerge when you think about this may help you understand the emotional fracture that death creates. What would help you to deal with this fracture? Nothing, perhaps, except time. However, while time is passing, it often helps to be allowed to talk about it—to have a listener who will let you share events, memories, and stories over and over again while the healing process is taking place. You could help another by being that listener.

If I Had Only . . .

Regret can be a hammer that pounds pain into a good-bye, filling a heart with guilt, anger—sometimes depression. It's hard to forgive oneself, genuinely. But without forgiveness, grief caused by regret is hard to heal. Guilt and regret can numb certain parts of life, leading people to withdraw and do strange things. Regret is the sad realization that it's too late—for that relationship; for that person; for that period of life.

The girl who argued with her father before going to the party was tortured with regrets. So was the girl whose friend committed suicide and the mother who thought her son was killed by her own destructive example. It sometimes helps such people to remind them of what can be done to improve *present* relationships, or what can be done the next time, so other regrets can be avoided. The mother was reminded of all the other young boys and girls she had helped with drug problems—now that she was a drug counselor—and that her son in his love had forgiven her and wanted her now to forgive herself. Yes, the grief of the "If I had only . . ." is a warning to us all, while we still have time.

The Anger of the "Whys?"

Why should a young baby die? Why should a budding adolescent be killed in an accident? Why would a young man want to take his life? Why? It's hard to say good-bye when we shouldn't have to; when there is more of living to be done; when the circumstances seem unfair.

The premature end of a life seems tragic and unjust, especially if the life seems cut short needlessly. Somehow it seems easier to accept death when the person is elderly or has been sick for a long time. Part of the mystery of life and death is why some are given longer lives than others. Just as we are denied the reason for seemingly unjust deaths, so we are kept from knowing the pain the person might have had to endure later in life if he or she had lived. In the end, each person must answer the "Why did it happen?" with a personal spiritual or philosophical understanding of life. Perhaps you could help by assisting the other to think through such answers.

It Will Hurt Too Much

Grief is the cost of loving and caring. When fearing an anticipated "payment" for loving someone who is dying, we sometimes like to escape or avoid going through the wrenching emotions of loss. One student said she couldn't make herself visit her dying grandmother because it hurt too much to see her dying. One woman said, "I don't want to talk about death. I can't stand to think of anyone I love dying." Perhaps there is no deeper hurt a person has to bear in life. But look at the choices.

We can choose to make ourselves vulnerable to loss by caring about others, becoming deeply involved with them, tying our happiness to having them around. We live with them—we play; create; build meaning into life with them. When we make such an emotional commitment to a relationship, it is possible to be hurt. A friend can move away; a friendship can dissolve; a person can die. If that happens, you are left alone with memories and desires. The more we love, the more possible it is to be hurt.

Or we can choose to not let ourselves get involved. We can establish only superficial relationships with others. We can care casually, making sure our heart strings don't become entwined too deeply. This choice means that we never want to be concerned enough about another to take a chance at disappointment. If it doesn't matter, you think, then you'll be safe from being hurt.

Which choice makes us human? Which choice has the

greatest chance for happiness? Is a happy life void of any pain or loss? Or is an unhappy life one that is closed off from feelings? Painful as they might be at times, losses and memories make life significant. But this means you have to care enough, sometimes get hurt, for life to have real meaning. If you close people off, what makes life worth living? Eventually, this choice leads to nothing being important—including the avoidance of pain—and the price you pay is not being able to really live.

Sometimes it helps to remind a friend about these choices. Get your friend to think and talk about all the things that have been *added* to his or her life because of the loved one who has died. Try to get your friend to weigh the worth of those memories against the present grief, asking about the choices. Strangely, this can be comforting.

The Fear and Uncertainty of Tomorrow

What happens after death? What is the meaning of life, if it ends in death? What answers have you found for yourself to these and other questions about death? Finding the answers that have meaning for you can make it easier to say good-bye when you have to.

The subject of religion and philosophy always comes up during this session on death in peer counseling training. This isn't strange. Death is a spiritual event. What we believe and hope lies beyond our present life is what we turn to for comfort and support. Students with a strong religious faith don't seem as devastated by death as those without a strong faith, even when it has been a tragic death. Nor do these students live with the fear of death that haunts so many others. Those who believe in God can more easily accept, without understanding it, the unknown reason for death. We who have this faith believe there is a tomorrow to be lived while still alive and eventually a spiritual life after death. This does not remove the sadness and grief that comes with death, but it does help to eliminate the despair and fear.

The inner resources of a person are tested at the time of grief. While they are going through it, people find out what they do or don't believe. It helps to let them talk about their beliefs and doubts and to share what *you* believe. Sometimes students ask if they should talk about their religious faith, if they know the other doesn't have one. Of course you should. Sharing your positive beliefs may be a demonstration of caring, depending on how you share them. Do not persuade. Persuasion is not caring. A person may be eager to hear what helps you—what gives you strength. But let the other person decide whether these shared positive beliefs of yours apply to him or her. Diane said, "I don't have that kind of faith. I wish I did, but I don't." In her voice was a longing and a searching. The greatest enemy of life are the feelings of defeat and hopelessness. Any encouragement and hope you can offer may lead someone through the shadow of death to living a new day.

IT'S THE SMALL THINGS THAT MAKE A DIFFERENCE

Now let's turn to more specific suggestions of what you can do to help—the practical ways you can respond individually to the unique needs of a grieving person.

Have you ever been in a situation where people are looking at you and you started to cry—and you didn't have a tissue? Yes, I have even seen boys and men in this situation. Your misery is increased because your nose is running and there is nothing you can use to blow your nose. Then, almost hesitantly, someone comes to your rescue, gently putting a tissue in your hand. After a good blow, you feel much better. It is a small thing, but oh, how helpful! All this means we don't need big things done for us, just thoughtful things like a hug—or a tissue when we are sad. Most of these suggestions are small acts of kindness that take more thought than effort or time. These are things we all can do; see if you don't agree.

• *Do or Say Something.*

The fear of blundering often keeps us from saying or doing anything. Awkwardness and embarrassment arise because we know there is nothing we can do to bring back the life that is gone. Wanting to say something that will help, we often censor ourselves, afraid that what we say won't be said well—might make the person feel worse. Wanting to avoid making a mistake, we often err by doing nothing. An awkward contact is more meaningful than a feeling of being abandoned through no contact or indifference.

When a person needs comfort, it is not a time to be selfish or worry about the kind of impression *you* will make. At such a time, what would you want done? When you have decided what this is, do the same for another! Just following my father's funeral, I returned to my work with two of my close colleagues. As I walked in that first morning, both greeted me, but neither one said a thing about my father's death. At first I was stunned, and then hurt. I wanted and needed them to say *something.* This made me realize I couldn't remember *what* other friends had said or written to console me, the words they had used, but I did remember that they had in some way said something.

The lesson I learned from this is that when you are grieving you aren't evaluating the words people use. You are listening to the feelings being expressed. You *do* hear the silences. It doesn't matter how sympathy is expressed, as long as it *is* expressed and is sincere. Even our stumbling words or one-sentence notes are enough.

• *Say Something Honest.*

There is no one "right" way to express your sympathy. Some prefer to talk directly to the grieving person; others would rather call on the phone, write a note, or send a card. Some express their concern with a hug, kiss, or clasp of a hand—or just by being there with the other and not saying anything. Letting the person cry in your presence without it making you uncomfortable can say a lot—or even crying with him or her if such tears are genuine.

What is said or written doesn't have to be elaborate or long, but it does have to be honest. It's also important not to avoid the reality of the death in what you say. Simple words, such as, "I'm sorry," "I know you are sad," or, "I'm sad because I miss him, too," are all that is needed. Don't be afraid to mention the person who has died by name. Your friend wants you to, especially if you knew him or her personally. Such comments as, "I'll always remember him for. . ."; "He meant so much to me"; "It was such fun when she and I did . . ." can be a comfort. Ask what you can do to help, or ask if your friend wants to talk about it. I often refer to my own source of comfort by saying, "I'm praying for you," or "I've asked God to comfort you." Even those who do not refer to God frequently will not reject this or be hurt by such a message.

• *Find a Way to Be Helpful.*

Death often comes suddenly, even when expected. It is a shock. As the mind absorbs the reality, often the person is disoriented, not thinking about or interested in physical matters. But people still need to eat; children need to be cared for; people need to be notified and arrangements made. Some of these things you can't do, but you could make it possible for others to do them. What about taking the casserole your mother made to the grieving neighbor? Could you help entertain any of the younger children? What errands could be run? If it is a school friend, could you offer to pick up his or her homework or take notes in class you share during the time he or she is absent? And perhaps you can show support by going to the funeral or memorial service.

Let's stop a minute and talk about funerals and memorial services. Lots of families now are choosing the memorial service instead of a funeral. This is a service that celebrates the memory of the one who has died. Often family members or close friends participate, expressing their feelings and appreciation for the one being honored. The kind of ritual, service, or final "good-bye" should be decided and designed by the family itself. Such activities and rituals, including preparation for them, can be a source of the comfort loved ones need. It gives a family something concrete to do while their minds and hearts get used to the realization a loved one is dead. Some have to see the person dead before this happens. Others don't need this, or want it, but the service itself helps to bring acceptance that this is the final good-bye. Matthew couldn't go to his grandfather's funeral, and now, almost two years later, what he really needs for comfort is to be able to go back to Michigan to see his grandfather's grave. He could then say good-bye.

It may be difficult or, we think, impossible to make ourselves attend a funeral or memorial service—even if we are physically able to. If we refuse to go, we are denying a friend our care. It means a lot to see one's friends gathering to express their care to the family over their loss. Some families even stand at the door after the service to greet those who have come—and to thank them. It's all right to show your tears as you speak to them. That, too, is comforting. Your presence that day may be the most helpful thing you, individually, can do.

• Take Time to Listen.

People who are grieving need and want to talk. It may be a way of letting go of emotions or attempting to hold on to the one who is gone. But too often we give subtle or not so subtle messages to the person in grief that we don't want to hear about the details or his or her feelings. Even if we are close to a friend, death often seems to make us feel uncomfortable.

This is why the woman said she didn't want to talk about death—that it was going to give her a headache if she continued. She failed to see, though, how the talking was helping those who had experienced death. Feelings were being released. Their grief seemed less painful by being able to share with others who were listening with feelings. Often, leaders in peer counseling dread this session, because they fear the emotions that may be expressed. They are afraid they won't know what to do with these feelings or how to be helpful to those expressing these feelings.

It *may* be painful for you to listen, but so what? If talking helps someone, then do you care enough to make yourself listen? Open the door for them by simply asking if they would like to talk. Or, you can mention the person in your conversation and see if your friend picks up the invitation to talk. Sometimes grieving people don't want to talk. Some people can't handle their emotions. But that's all right— you've given them a chance if they want to take it.

This is particularly important when someone is suffering from regrets or guilt. Encourage that person to talk without any reaction, rejection, or judgment. It is unkind to deny the guilt or regrets a person feels by telling the person he or she shouldn't feel that way. There *are* reasons why we should feel guilty, and we do! Being told not to can almost make it worse. I think we can help, though, by focusing on what can be done from this point on. It is too late to make amends to the one who died, but based on our mistakes, we can do things differently in the future. Try to give the person some hope and some basis for rebuilding damaged and bruised self-respect.

You don't have to have an answer or a solution, but you do need to listen unflinchingly. Perhaps you can react with questions that will lead your friend to think of what actions can be taken to prevent similar tragedies or help repair the lives of others who have no one to help. Much guilt has been healed by becoming involved in the problems of others.

• *Help When Days Get Lonely.*

When the service is over, the relatives have gone home, the flowers are beginning to fade, and there is nothing more to do that demands your attention, then the real grief and loneliness set in. Even the notes, cards, and calls have stopped and one is left with meals to prepare and routine living to be done. The time comes when you really need a friend to talk to, an invitation to dinner, an unexpected note, a picnic at the beach, or someone to stop by for a brief time each evening. The conversation can be casual, short or long, about what is happening so far with your friend or even about the lasting memories of the loved one.

A fifth-grade boy had been killed in an accident at an amusement park. It was a crushing blow to a close friend because the two of them had done so many things together. At times, when he talked with his parents, Nathan revealed that his loss had been the hardest thing he had gone through. A couple of months later, he announced to his father that he was going down to visit the mother of his friend. He thought she must be lonely without her son and it might make her feel better to have a visit with him. So he did this, and they visited for a short while. When he left, the mother gave Nathan a gift of a poster that had been her son's favorite. She may not have said thanks to Nathan in so many words, but she did through her gift of the poster. What an example he set for all of us!

There is no set schedule for grieving or predetermined time it takes to move through it. People go through this experience in different ways. Some people don't cry until months or even years after the death. Some get rid of everything that can remind them of their loved one; others keep things around as happy memories. Some remember loved ones through memorials that are set up, gifts to cancer and heart research, planting of trees, scholarship donations, and similar things. These gifts are living memorials because they add to the lives of those who are still living.

What this all means is that our help and comfort must be adjusted to the needs and desires of the grieving. Some need help a year later more than at the immediate time of death.

Some want flowers at the funeral or on the altar at a church service in memory of a loved one; some appreciate more a donation given on the anniversary of the death.

Betty died quite suddenly from a brain tumor in her early fifties. She was my first neighbor when I got married, so she taught me many things I needed to know. Through the early years as neighbors, we spent birthdays, holidays, and special occasions together as couples. The last time I saw her was on Christmas Eve—a month before she died. I didn't cry at her funeral, or later when I went to see her husband a month after she was buried. On her birthday, I put flowers on her grave. Then I cried and said my goodbye. She really isn't gone, because I think of her when I pick up a recipe she gave me or use the Christmas tree skirt or napkin rings she made for me. Through these gifts and memories, she has become a lasting part of my life.

THE WOUNDS THAT ARE HARD TO HEAL

Suicide is an ever-present part of most discussions about death. Such deaths leave deep wounds. Death that comes this way hurts loved ones because it seems the person has found life too painful to be lived and sought release through death. Whenever this happens, I feel that I, among others, have failed because I haven't done enough to make this a caring world for that person. This guilt is what makes it so agonizing for those close to the person who has taken his or her life. What follows is a deep self-condemnation that is intensified by what some think is the silent criticism and judgment of others. The survivors of suicide deaths, particularly the family, need special help from others. How to give such help is often a hard question to answer.

The most helpful explanation of suicide I know was given to me by a psychiatrist friend. She said that she learned from working with emotional problems that people differ in their ability to throw off emotional stress, just as people differ in their ability to throw off physical illness. Some are born with greater emotional resilience and strength than others. Such people find their emotional wounds heal, and heal rapidly. Others are almost constantly in emotional pain. Sometimes the pain becomes too great and defeats their courage to go on, just as physical pain can do. Some combat this stress with a strong spiritual faith, others by a commitment to a purpose for living. Many battle it by knowing their life is needed by someone else. Others don't have any of these resources.

What I'm trying to say is that one's emotional will to live can wear out, just as the body does. Some people feel they can no longer continue living. The family is not at fault, nor friends, nor others who may have tried to help. Perhaps the events and circumstances of life have taken a greater toll on the more fragile emotional health of the person than it has on others. Loved ones need help in understanding this, so they can deal with the shock and guilt of suicide more constructively. They need help in sorting through their confusion and condemnation. Perhaps they might be led to realize that their loved one no longer has to suffer. This would be comforting.

There is something we can do to help prevent a suicide. Few people take their lives if they know and believe that they are *needed* by someone, particularly someone who is not related. When people feel their lives are important to another person, that their dying would be a severe loss to that friend, this emotional tie can keep them alive. But if we are that friend, we have to tell them they mean this much to us. It isn't enough, or even helpful, to say to the one considering death, "You don't really want to die." At this time, he or she may actually want to. But if you can say honestly, "I don't want you to die; I need you," this message may be heard and believed, and a life may be saved.

But if a friend does take his or her life, don't condemn yourself. We are human. We are not divine. We make mistakes. We might have done more for the person. If we failed to do what we could, what can we learn for the next time? If we did what we thought we should, can we forgive our shortcomings and mistakes? Let's try, and let's try to help others do the same.

KEEP FOR REMINDERS

This has been a difficult chapter for me to write. You can't talk and think about death without touching some sensitive memories or reopening some sadness. In talking with you, I have relived some of my experiences with death and remembered the sadness of others. But I've also renewed my commitment to life. I hope it has done some of this for you.

Some of what I've said may be hard for you to understand or even think about. But at some point you will have the opportunity to use it to help someone who is going through the experience of the death of a loved one. It happens to us all. Keep what I have said. Turn to it when you want help yourself or want to help someone else who is saying good-bye to a friend.

9

Priceless Gifts from Real Friends

The evening had arrived. The tables were dressed with soft yellow tablecloths and baskets of fresh flowers. The aroma of the prime rib cooking floated in from the cafeteria kitchen. The PA system was working. Then the guests began arriving, escorted by their peer counselor hosts and hostesses, looking very adult in their lovely dresses and neat shirts and ties. All were gathering for the Palo Alto Peer Counseling Recognition Dinner. Each student had invited an adult guest who had had an important influence on his or her life. After dinner, students would introduce their guests, thanking them for the contribution each had made to their lives.

What a moving experience! The guests included Boy Scout leaders, a pastor, elementary school teachers, a school counselor, former neighbors, brothers and sisters, and many dads and moms. As each student nervously stood before the 250 people gathered, stammering out words of appreciation, everyone there was touched by what was happening. Some guests were amazed to learn that they had been that important. Some cried. Most simply beamed with great appreciation. By the words of the students and the evidence of their lives, the adults were hearing the story of the power of their gifts of love and care.

As you read the "happy endings" to the story of the priceless gift of being a real friend to yourself and others, there are several things I want you to remember:

First, the results I am going to tell you about are not made up, nor are they exaggerated. As you have read the book, studied the skills, done the exercises (I hope), and thought about your life and relationships with others, you may think it all makes sense—but does it really work? Could you really do those things, and if you did would it make any difference? The only thing I can say to that is that you have to find out for yourself—you have to try doing these things and see what happens. I know it has worked for many and the results have been significant.

Second, the quotes and incidents that I have included have come from students and adults who have been involved in peer counseling. They attribute what has happened to them and others to first getting the training and then having the opportunities to use this training in helping others. It is important to remember that the prime focus of peer counseling training is *to reach out to others*. There are many support and self-help programs around, but the main purpose of these programs is to provide help for the individuals in the program. Peer counseling stresses getting involved with others—not just turning inward.

Third, this means that getting involved with others—helping someone else—is the necessary factor in actually learning how to be a real friend. It is the old principle of learning by doing. I can't "assign" you, the reader, a person to help. You will have to find that person or persons yourself. If you want to become the kind of friend you would like to have, you can only learn by doing. You have to *practice* your caring skills before they can become part of who you are.

Finally, the process starts with each one of you deciding what it is about yourself you want or need to change to be a real friend. Then, you learn how to change. You put your new skills and habits into practice by reaching out to others.

You discover that the best way to help yourself is to help others who need you. This cycle will be illustrated as students speak to you in their words and through their experiences.

BECOMING THE FRIEND

Most people who need help have to change something to solve their problems—change themselves or change what they are doing. It is hard often to realize this and very painful to admit these faults or inadequacies to someone else. Because this is true, it is important that those who want to help others are able to do this themselves. Why should you expect someone else to tell you about their problems or what they are doing wrong, if you aren't able or willing to do this also? We need to experience the *feeling* of exposing our weaknesses to someone else in order to be more understanding of another's struggles. To reveal one's problems takes courage—or desperation! Early in peer counseling training, students are encouraged and supported in exploring what they want to change about themselves. I asked you to do something similar to this in Chapter 6. Here are some examples of what students have said they want to change:

"I want to learn how to meet people more easily . . . that's one of the reasons I took this class."

"I think I'd like to change my relationship with my father."

"I think the most important thing for me to change is getting a clearer idea of my values and what I want to do."

"I'd like to change my competitiveness. I've been told by a friend that I compete with her . . . in sports or academically or when she says something wrong. Then I use it against her in some way to make myself a better person and make her a lesser person. And that's something I'd like to work on."

"I'd like to be less sensitive with people I'm close to. Once in a while I find I overreact or am too sensitive and I'd like not to do that . . . kind of keep my balance more."

"I'd like to learn how to say no when I don't want to do something with a friend. Sometimes I lie to get out of it . . . and I don't like that about myself."

"I'd like to get over being jealous of my sister."

Scott went even further when he said:

"The thing I would like to change is that earlier in my life, I was kind of withdrawn and shy and I find now that I missed a lot of relationships with people that . . . I felt could have been special. Now I'd like to change this in the future. I'd like to be able to come up to somebody and say, 'My name is Scott . . .' and go through my qualities. Then if I had something in common, I'd like to develop the relationship not only around that, but about different qualities and to develop myself and also the person I'm talking to . . ."

It would be helpful to you, if you haven't already done this, to go some place where you can be alone and undisturbed and honestly explore what you want to change about yourself that would make a difference in your life. No one finds this easy to do, to take off the layers of protection that we put on to hide our faults and weaknesses. But if others have had the courage and determination to do this, I'll wager that you can do it, too. You know, once you've done this, you may actually begin to make the changes.

The Training Helps You Do It

The training to become a peer counselor, what we have been going over in this book, provides the knowledge of what you can do to change and become a real friend to yourself and others. Some students are skeptical when they begin training, just as you still may be. They wonder how relevant it will be and what meaning it can have for them.

High school students in a private school in California came to training with those questions. Many had failed at other schools; some of them had family relationships that were a disaster; a few had run away; some were heavily into drugs; one had been in and out of prison. Some found it impossible to connect with any group. Most lived with self-hatred. Their teacher led them to learn how to trust; how to ask questions; how to listen to one another; how to put themselves in someone else's place; and finally, how to help one another. Halfway through their training the oldest and toughest boy in the class was seen eating lunch with an eighth grader who was not in the class. He was a frail, nervous boy with a tic and awkward coordination. Up to this time, no one had wanted to be seen with him, let alone eat with him. But his new friend took him under his big senior-on-campus wing. Then other students began being nice to him. He began to smile and relax. He had found a *real* friend.

The happy ending is that so did the senior boy—he found *himself* a friend. He was needed; he was admired for good reasons. He could now like himself. He had become the friend he had always wanted for himself.

When students are asked if they feel the training has changed them in any way, the answers are varied. Sandy said her life had been enriched. She now feels more self-confidence and significance. Rich said he now is better able to be open with another individual about himself. Andy felt that he had become more patient. Paul said, "I am more aware of discomfort, both my own and that of others, and I feel better equipped to discover the source of the discomfort." Susan said, "I definitely have more confidence in myself as a result of the program. This was probably because I found myself helping others. In helping peers, I learned more about myself."

Often students keep in touch with the program after they leave high school. As they write or talk about their lives as young adults, they reflect on what the continuing benefits have been for them. When Allen was in law school, he wrote,

> I have gotten to know far more people intimately and, as a result, see much that we have in common as people. I feel as if I belong in with my peers—something I did not feel as a high school student. I feel much more secure.

Mark, writing from college, said,

> The training and the assignments have enabled me to see my strengths and accept my weaknesses. As a result of peer counseling, I care more for others and myself, accept others and myself, and have the tools and the strengths to help others and myself.

How wonderful it would be if you could feel and say the same things about yourself two years from now. It *is* worth making the effort!

The Change Is Gradual, But It's Happening

When students begin applying their caring skills in their lives all around them, they are often not aware of how they are changing because the change occurs so gradually. But their friends, parents, and teachers are aware of what is happening. As one boy said, "I've become a lot more sensitive. People notice it in me and say, 'Hey, you used to be kind of mean, but now you're really nice!'" One tenth-grade girl said:

> I've grown with peer counseling since the eighth grade, and the ideas that are taught have become a part of the way I act. I can't say whether I would have done these things without it or not—most likely not.

Sometimes people don't notice the gradual changes of habits, ways of reacting to people, feelings about self and others, until they themselves consciously or unconsciously use them. Here is a vivid example of this happening:

Stephanie was a pom-pom girl, a good student, and friendly, vivacious, and warm. She agreed to try and help a classmate who was considered "strange" by other students in this school. His actions often brought laughter—*at* him—and certainly one wouldn't want to run around with him! Stephanie, however, was willing to help. She began showering him with friendliness, spending time each week to talk with him alone and always saying "hi" to him and going up to him if she saw him in the hall.

One day, when they were talking alone, the boy awkwardly told her the kids were beginning to say that Stephanie was his girl friend. She reacted by turning red. Then she took a deep breath, starting to lift her finger to wave in his face while she lowered the boom. Just as the words "now listen here, let's get this straight" rose to her lips, she caught herself. Releasing her breath, she put down her finger, paused, and gently said, "Well, that's interesting. Do *you* think I'm your girl friend?" When the boy looked down and quietly stammered a no, Stephanie asked, "What *do* you think is our relationship?" After thinking awhile, her "friend" forced out the admission that he knew she was trying to help him. As he talked, he even got the courage to tell her things he didn't like about himself, and how he would like to be different.

Do you think that would have happened if Stephanie had reverted to her usual way of behaving when she was angry with someone? She knew as she talked about this how much she would have hurt him if she had but admitted that she couldn't have done the helpful thing before her training. "Instead, I would have been really cruel . . . and that is what everyone was doing to him. But I was able to stop—and really be a friend to him. I'm not sure I will remember this the next time, but I feel good about what I did." Another student put it this way:

I feel my caring skills training has been a major positive force in my life. Although the trend is slow moving, it is still there within me. I feel this training will
still be changing me ten years from now.

Yes, I feel good about what I did, or I got much more
satisfaction from being kind and caring than I did if I had
been cruel. In so many different ways, both of these students were saying what they hoped they would remember
the next time—that they are the ones who benefit when
they are a real friend. Kevin said it a different way:

I used to think that some people were better than
others. Now I hold the view that people are just different from each other, rather than being better or worse.
My work with this caring assignment helped me to
develop a different philosophy.

As you read what these students have said and done,
maybe you are beginning to realize why it is so important to
you and your growth to actually find out what it is like to
try and help someone. Even if your efforts don't help the
other, your attempts will help *you*—even if they only make
clear what you still need to learn. But most of the time,
when a person works at meeting another's personal needs,
extending a hand literally or figuratively, miracles happen
to both the one helped and the one who offered the help.

BEING THE FRIEND

When someone genuinely learns to care it can't be self-
contained. It spills over, gradually seeping into the lives of
others who need friendship and care. This happens usually
in small, almost imperceptible ways. Allen expressed his belief that he had helped his friends mostly through listening
and guiding them to seeing alternatives.

I don't look upon this as counseling so much as being a friend enough to care and knowing enough not
to order remedies for them. We have talked about get-

ting along with people, sex, career choice, drugs, and getting along with oneself.

Caring enough to show people that they matter in whatever situation you meet them *is* being a real friend. When more and more of you care this way, schools will be more pleasant to attend; homes will be places where you want to be.

The potential for this happening was demonstrated in an eastern suburban high school where a peer counseling program had been functioning for three years. In surveying a random sample of the student body and asking the peer counselors to fill out questionnaires, it was found that the seventy peer counselors had only worked with 69 "assigned counselees," mostly dealing with academic problems. However, they had given informal services to 301 students in the school, and these informal contacts focused on personal problems for the most part. It is also interesting that 60 percent of these informal contacts had resulted from self-referrals, 26 percent from contacts initiated by a peer counselor, and the remainder from casual referrals by others. This says to me that most of these seventy peer counselors could do what an eleventh-grade boy said he could do in a California school:

> I can now pick up hints that someone wishes to speak to me or needs attention. Furthermore, I can now respond to people who look depressed or upset.

It also may mean that these students showed by the way they treated others and by a genuine warmth and friendliness that it was all right to approach them and ask for help. Fellow students saw them as caring people. Perhaps they expressed in various ways what another student said about the peer counseling training:

> Not only do I understand myself better, but I am not so quick to judge people. I am not as superficial. There is so much learning to be done in a deeper, more meaningful way. The topics discussed [which

have been covered in this book] are important in everyday life. The skills I learned will stay with me for the rest of my life.

In the spring of 1982, money was raised with the help of peer counselors to give a caring student award scholarship to a boy and girl from each of the two high schools in Palo Alto. Members of the senior classes were asked to nominate students they felt exemplified a caring student and tell why. From these nominations, the four students were chosen.

Those chosen had not sought to get recognition for the caring, humble acts they had done throughout their high school life. They even were overwhelmed when they learned of the award, Lisa saying that she did not see herself as that kind of a person. Others had, however. Every extra moment she had, she spent helping in the Educable Mentally Handicapped class or doing something with these students. She went along on the ski trip when this class went up to the mountains, helping students get up when they had fallen, encouraging them to try. Even though she was the star pitcher on the girl's softball team, she often offered to take other positions so that other teammates might have a chance to play.

One student writing his recommendation for Ned said, "I don't even know the guy, but every time I see him, he's helping someone." Ned's whole purpose, even at his early age, is to be helpful to others, to make the school and the world a kinder place. He often spends time thinking about ways to do this. Whenever he spoke his classmates listened because they knew he *lived* what he said.

Similar things could be said about the other two. But all four of these students knew they wanted to be real friends to those who didn't have a friend, and they looked for opportunities to do this.

GIVING THE PRICELESS GIFT

Sometimes students can only get the courage to start using their new skills by being asked to help another. When they accept these assignments what happens often amazes them and impresses many adults. They are faithful, persistent, patient, and sometimes discouraged. But most never give up—and they don't even though they do this on their own time, without pay or school credit. I think you will enjoy reading about some of the priceless gifts that have been given by some of these young people.

BARBARA

Barbara was the first friend Meg, a hard-of-hearing classmate, had ever had. Meg had lived in a fantasy world of her own creation. She had become afraid of contacts with living people. She needed a living real friend, and Barbara agreed to try. So she asked Meg to meet her for lunch. Meg agreed, but never showed up. After making several attempts to find her, Barbara realized Meg was hiding from her because she was afraid. So she kept trying and finally "cornered" Meg for a lunch one day; eventually they ate lunch together almost regularly. As this continued, Meg began to unfold like a flower. She talked to Barbara; she talked to her teachers—and eventually to other students. Then the family moved away. It was a painful good-bye for Meg to leave her first and real friend, Barbara, but she kept in contact through many letters. In writing, she thanked Barbara for this friendship and for teaching her that she could make and keep other friends.

MARIA

Johnny sat talking to his counselor while he enrolled in another new high school. He lived with his mother, and they had moved almost every year. This might have given him enough problems, but he also had a brain tumor and had lost much of his hair because of the chemotherapy. He was also blind in one eye. With a pleading look on his face and a crack in his voice, he said to his counselor, "I want a *friend.*"

So the counselor asked Maria to help. She had had her own problems and wanted more friends herself. After getting to know Johnny, she spent much of her free time doing things with him. She gradually got discouraged because Johnny never seemed to show any indication that the friendship meant anything to him, or that it was helping him to be happier. Finally, with the help of his counselor, she realized that Johnny didn't know yet *how* to return her friendship. He'd never had a friend before. So she didn't give up. Then Johnny's health got worse, and it seemed he would not have long to live. He had told her that he had always dreamed of going to Hawaii, but there would never be enough money to do this. So Maria organized a collection of money to send Johnny to Hawaii before he died. As he was leaving, choking back his tears, he said to his counselor, "I *did* find a friend at Sentinel." The happiest of endings is that although Johnny did not return to that school because his mother moved again, he didn't die. His tumor stopped growing and he was given more years to find new friends.

ALLEN

Allen gave a priceless gift to a fourth-grade boy who was athletic and a fighter. In fact, the only way he would deal with his classmates was to fight them. Each day, he made a trip to the office, or home, because of a fight. Allen was not athletic, nor did he look like an athlete. He was slight of build, very serious and academic. When asked if he would work with Ron, Allen looked shocked and said, "I'm hardly athletic; I don't believe I qualify." Assured that he wasn't expected to be athletic, that he was to use his own approach to problems, that he just had to be himself and use his skills, Allen finally agreed. He got Ron to talk about what he was trying to get by fighting. Then he suggested other ways to get the same thing. A couple of weeks after he first met Ron, Ron's teacher heard him say to his classmates on the playground, "You know there are other ways to get what you want besides fighting." The fighting began to disappear. Then Ron's father called the school and said he did not want his son to see Allen any longer. It turned out that the father, a former professional football player, didn't like the change in his son. He wanted Ron to be a fighter. So Allen had to say good-bye. He had come to care for Ron and it hurt him that he could no longer see him. In trying to console Allen, I told him that he had planted a seed of new behavior in Ron's life that no one could ever take away from him. He now knew that he could get what he wanted from classmates, friends, and adults—without fighting.

Each time I remember these young people who did give the kind of friendship they wanted for themselves, I feel moved, hopeful, and enriched. There are many more such examples I could relate, but I think you now have a glimpse of the power of the priceless gifts from real friends. There are still two more I want to tell, however, because they show the chain reaction that happens when people learn how to care.

THE RIPPLES OF CARING THAT FLOW ON

One night after I finished a talk on peer counseling, a woman stood up and said she just had to tell what had happened to her daughter. They had moved to Palo Alto when their handicapped daughter was a sophomore in high school. Mimi only went to the school half days and was placed in the special education class for handicapped students. Early that year, Mimi was given a peer counselor to help her with her social adjustments and problems. This student worked faithfully to teach her many things about interpersonal relationships. "Now my daughter is in college and thinks of herself as a nonhandicapped, normal girl. She also is reaching out to help her college classmates, most of whom do not have any physical disability. She is happy and productive. I can never say enough thanks to that peer counselor and to the program that rescued our daughter."

There is a second ending to the story. Janet, as a high school junior, took peer counseling training the first year the program began. After her training, she agreed to work with Mimi. When Janet graduated from high school, she decided she wanted to become a teacher of the physically disabled. After her education and training, she returned to Palo Alto to become the teacher of the same class where she had worked with Mimi as a peer counselor. A few years later, Janet enrolled in a peer counseling adult leadership class, to prepare herself as a peer counseling leader. In addition to volunteering her time as a leader, she also teaches the training to her disabled students.

As Janet reflects on that first assignment, she realizes that Mimi had a lot of social problems when she was in high school. She wasn't making friends; she tended to be pretty demanding of other people at times—and she wasn't able to express her feelings. "I think it was very good for her to learn how to express those feelings, just as I now see this in my own class of physically disabled students. They lack communication skills, even the basic skills most kids have from day one."

This is a beautiful illustration of the powerful ripple effects of caring for another—what it does for that person, as well as oneself. Helping Mimi led to helping others. It also led Janet's life career and finally the full circle back to her teaching other friendless students how to be real friends to others.

Here is another example, perhaps less dramatic but also very meaningful, that provided a priceless gift to an adult:

Todd was a young math teacher in a junior high school that had shifted from an all-white, upper-class, college-bound student body to one in which minorities were represented. As he was taking the leadership training he expressed his depression about the behavior of his students, their apathy about learning, and his relationship to them. He was constantly weary. He didn't know what to do, and he didn't feel that this peer counseling training would work with the students in his classes. "How could I possibly take time out, anyway, from teaching math to try and teach this? I hardly have time to cover what I'm supposed to now," he often questioned with anger.

He returned to his class, but things got worse. He dreaded starting the second semester. He considered taking a leave of absence. Then he decided he had nothing to lose by trying some of the peer counseling skills training. So he put away the math and spent the first two weeks of the semester teaching some of the caring skills we have covered.

When I saw him several months later, he was eager to tell me what had happened. It had worked! Students had changed their attitudes and behavior to one another and to him. He had changed! He saw them in a different way. He now looked forward to going to class. Then, he admitted sheepishly, "They have already covered the math they should have at this point in the year, despite the fact we gave up those two weeks. We aren't spending as much time fighting one another. We're working together!" From his eyes and his words, I knew that he had found the power of caring.

We as individuals really don't want to fight with one another or be competitive or hurt others. When we learn how to act in caring ways and use what we have learned, our lives will be changed! The first act leads to another, and then a whole chain has been started. I've known many people who were once self-centered and cruel who became caring people—but I've never know a caring person revert to a noncaring one. Doesn't this say volumes about the rewards that come from being a true, real friend to others?

HAVING A REAL FRIEND—BEING A FRIEND

Most of the human hungers you have—to be loved, to be important to someone, to be appreciated and cared about—won't be satisfied by seeking them directly. That which you seek, however, may come to you when you give it to others. This is what many of the students I've mentioned have shared with you. Those who have risked this challenge have found more than any of them expected.

The experience of having a real friend is always prior to

the experience of being a friend. As Shakespeare said, "Love, loving not itself, none other can." We may have to learn how to be a real friend to ourselves before we can become the friend we want to have. But if we make the effort, through peer counseling groups (or by reading this book) or in one of the many other possible ways to learn, we may find the "transforming friendship" that changes our lives and those of many, many others.

Everyone who has been involved in some way with the concepts I have presented to you through all these pages knows more of what it means to love one another—and themselves. Many young people are now, in small and in dramatic ways, using their lives to help those they now call friends. There are a lot more people out there, though, who need a real friend. Will you become that friend?

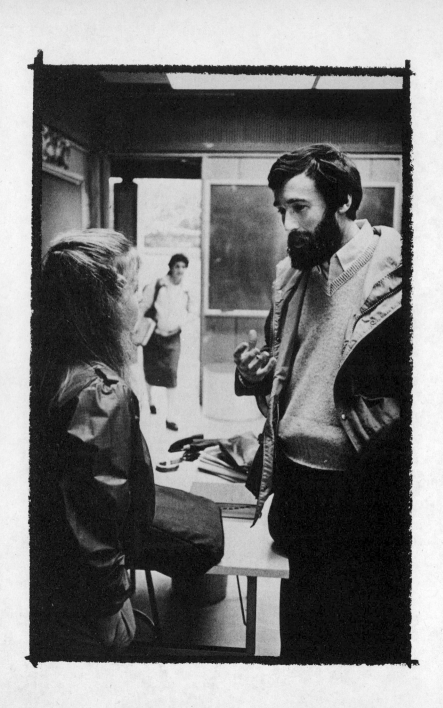

10

///////

Peer Counseling:
Teaching How to
Become a Real Friend

The core of the peer counseling program is the education of the heart. Just as a bird needs two wings to fly, so also a human being needs the education of the mind but also the education of the heart. We all probably agree that this is true, but teaching people how to care, to love, and to be a real friend, is severely neglected or haphazardly done in many schools and homes across our country. This accounts in part for why so many boys and girls feel as though they are zeros—unimportant to anyone. We can prevent this from happening. Young people can be taught to value themselves and to care about others. They also represent a vast human resource that has been underutilized in providing real friendship to all the lonely, unhappy people around them, including their families.

This basic message is what I give to adults as I start my adult leadership training to prepare them to become peer counseling leaders and teachers. This leadership training is what I recommend to schools, churches, and agencies wanting to implement a peer counseling program. The training proceeds by having adults experience the training provided to students, with appropriate adaptations for adults. Many people who have taken this training have indicated and expressed their own need for their hearts to be educated. The same skills taught to students are relevant to them, too, in their personal and professional work.

The main purpose for writing this book was to provide a resource for self-instruction that young people could use if they don't have an opportunity to participate in a formal peer counseling program. However, it may stimulate adults to explore the possibility of starting such a program. Although I can't conduct a leadership training in one chapter of a book, I can summarize some of the relevant information a person might want or need in order to explore the potential of beginning a program. More details can be obtained by writing to me.

PHILOSOPHY OF THE PROGRAM

The "program" is three things: 1) a *training* for students and leadership training for adults; 2) a personal *intervention,* or way of getting help for oneself; and 3) a *service* to others. The emphasis, as I said when I began, is the education of the heart as well as the head. Since the training is based on a developed curriculum, with specific skills taught in each session, the mind has to be involved. However, much time is spent in helping students to think about others rather than themselves; on giving to others one's time, skill, and concern; and on motivating students to notice people around them who are being hurt or neglected. Although students and some leaders would like the training sessions to become group counseling, this is not the purpose of the training.

As students are taught caring and interpersonal skills, they do learn positive ways to cope with developmental tasks and interpersonal expectations and needs. In this way, the training does provide a helpful intervention for young people who are in a difficult period of their lives. However, every skill is taught in the context of how students can use these skills to help others.

The goals of the training are to prepare students to work with and help peers who are lonely, shy, or shut off from normal peer relationships because of physical or mental handicaps or those who have undeveloped social skills. Students are not trained to work with problems that demand professional skill and knowledge. The course work itself, including the practicing that is part of the course, is effective. But it has been demonstrated that students learn far more when they actually apply these skills in some way in their everyday lives or in helping someone they have been asked to help.

THE PROGRAM'S FRAMEWORK

As I describe the framework of the program, I will be talking about the Palo Alto (California) School District program. Many other programs exist throughout the country that differ from this one, with variations in types of training, curriculum, age of students involved, and setting. Quite a number of these programs, however, have been based on the Palo Alto model.

Personnel

The Palo Alto program is designed to train students between grades 7 and 12 in all four secondary schools. These students help and work with other students in their own schools as well as in elementary schools in the district. This means that a coordinating staff is necessary. As director of the program, I have two coordinating staff members, Pam Boyers and James Toole.

Students are "recruited" or invited to take peer counseling training when we visit classes or talk to groups. Often students sign up for training based on word-of-mouth comments of classmates or brothers and sisters who have been in the program. This means that we do not screen students for the training. Anyone can take it, irrespective of their qualifications, problems, or assets. In this way many students have received help for themselves under the guise of learning how to help others—receiving help with a unique kind of dignity. Often students have said when completing their training that it should be a required course before graduation, and then added, "but then, that would ruin it."

Opportunities for Training

Originally the only way students could take the training was to sign up for one of the small group classes that were scheduled after school or in the evening, meeting once a week for twelve weeks, or a total of eighteen hours. These groups are about ten to twelve in size, taught by two trained volunteer adults. Classes are scheduled at each of the four schools. We find, however, that boys are underrepresented in these groups because they conflict with after-school sports and jobs.

To expand the program, we initiated peer counseling as an elective class that meets daily for one full semester as part of the regular school day. These classes are the normal class size and are taught by a credentialed teacher who has previously taken the adult leadership training. This method of providing training allows time to cover more material and to learn the skills. Also, it has proven to be a way of getting more boys involved.

In the fall of 1981 a third method of training was introduced in the high schools. Juniors and seniors were invited to take a weekend training followed by semiweekly evening sessions for two months focused on providing help and friendship to students in the new freshman class. Each trained peer counselor volunteered to "look after" three to five of these ninth graders, getting to know them, helping them with problems, and alerting the counseling staff regarding any problems they saw beginning. Approximately fifty students eventually were trained.

There are several significant advantages to this third method of preparing young people to be real friends to others. First, it provides students an opportunity to get the training without having to make a long-term commitment of time. Young people are often very busy, and most of their out-of-school hours are chock-full of obligations. For some it is very difficult to find a day they could be available for twelve weeks, even though they might want to.

Second, by offering the training in a concentrated period, students are giving up their free time, but not on a long-term basis. It does seem that there is a difference in the spirit and quality of the training when it is done on their own time. Once they are trained—and convinced—they *find* the time to be involved. Often we underestimate the power of giving something without getting back a tangible reward. Young people are idealistic, and they do respond when that idealism is challenged and focused.

Third, having a specific focus for the training, such as being a friend to a freshman, makes the training immediately more relevant. Always in the back of their minds as they are learning is the question, How can I use this with the students I will be assigned? Students met their freshmen friends after their first weekend of training. As the training continued throughout the following months, they had real, actual problems to deal with as they practiced learning more caring skills.

Finally, having a large group of peer counselors focused on a particular and recognized task brought about some ripple effects through the entire school. Many became sensitive to the cliques in the school and how they affected students. Some became more alert to the indifference that often exists in the social life of a school. Some students contacted these peer counselors on their own, for counsel about their problems. Teachers, administrators, and counselors began drawing on peer counselors' interpersonal skills in other ways— some of the peer counselors added further responsibilities by volunteering to help in the mentally handicapped class.

Any one of these training modes is effective. The one you

choose would depend on the different circumstances of the students and on the availability of adults to do the training. One word of caution, though. Always start with a small effort and do it well. Then you can expand as you learn, as the program is accepted, and as your demand for services increases.

THE CURRICULUM

Adults wanting to start such a program might need further guidelines. In fact, a program of this kind should be designed most carefully. Young people have had some sloppy experiments tried on them. In peer counseling training we follow a carefully tested curriculum that has been revised over the years based on our experiences. It is titled *Curriculum Guide for Student Peer Counseling Training* and is basically a guide for leaders, not a textbook for students. Much of the curriculum has been presented in this book, along with additional exercises and activities not included in the curriculum, such as the values memory journey. Some topics taught in peer counseling have not been touched on in this book, such as how to approach someone in authority, assertiveness, and how to talk to someone about a sensitive issue. Students do spend a session each on the topics of family concerns, health and drug problems, and boy-girl relationships—practicing how they can use their caring skills to help classmates with these problems. In doing this, they use their own problems as content material. In this way, they are learning as well as receiving help.

For this to be possible, for young people to be willing to reveal their problems and concerns to members of the group, group trust and cohesiveness has to be developed early in the training. Many students in peer counseling are needy themselves. Some are lonely; some have other needs. Often they come to peer counseling believing that this is a place where they can learn how to be a real friend—and how to make friends. This always thrills me because it means they are doing something positive to change their lives. However, if they are going to succeed at doing this, the group has to provide the atmosphere and the support that each person needs to learn how to change.

As trust develops in a training group, students begin to relate individual experiences of loneliness or to talk about their fears of neglect or rejection and about the friends they wished they had, eventually acknowledging their own desires about the kind of friend they want to be. As this happens, they are taught the suggestions and reminders discussed throughout this book. They practice using them on one another and are urged to try them with others outside the group. What happens when they do is discussed at each of the sessions. When needed, additional suggestions or support are given.

Students may develop a willingness to help, but they still need courage. Adolescents by nature are not very secure in most situations. Now they are being asked to try something that is quite different from their usual routine. They may want to believe what I say will happen when they try—but is it true? Sometimes it takes time to convince them. As the "pushing" continues with each session, gradually some are willing to do something. When they do, they are encouraged—even excited. Their mistakes are discussed. They are given encouragement when they get discouraged. Hearing what is happening, feeling the excitement someone is expressing, may give another the courage to try.

Important and Sensitive Topics

Two topics in the curriculum that are important yet sensitive ones, and therefore sometimes difficult to teach, are boy-girl relationships—or sexual issues—and death and dying. Both require that the leader be comfortable with the subjects and be careful how he or she handles the value issues that are part of both these topics. At this point in the training, the leader, if doing an effective job, will have become a significant person to the young people in the group. You can't teach this course effectively without believing what you are teaching and without practicing it in your own life—and that includes the care and help you give to your students. As you do, young people begin responding to you as an adult who really cares about them. With such a relationship, the values you promote or discourage can have a major influence on their lives. Teach your values, point out why you don't hold other values, but always in a way that shows consideration and acceptance of those held by others.

When teaching the lesson on sexual issues appropriate adaptations may have to be made depending on the age group you are teaching. Two lessons for this topic are included in the curriculum, one intended for junior high students and the other for high school students. In my experiences in teaching this lesson, I have found that students are not as concerned with the "heavy" issues of boy-girl relationships as they are with the simple, normal problems: What do you talk about on a date? What do I say to a boy if I don't want to hurt him but I don't want to dance with him? and How do you handle peer pressure and peer jealousy? Occasionally deeper concerns do come up, so if you have a hard time talking about sex in a healthy way, perhaps you shouldn't tackle this topic.

Death and dying is hard for a different reason. It is a topic that opens up sadness and memories of loved ones. It often is a sad session, with tears and possible agony. Sometimes you might not know how to handle this. At such times, let your heart tell you what to do.

Even though most peer counselors are young, many *have* experienced the death of a loved one. Some of these have been tragic experiences; others have been experiences that are barely remembered. But a general reaction to this session is appreciation because they don't have many chances to talk, think, and learn from others about death. This provides them an opportunity to talk about their misunder-

standings and fears. Many find it meaningful because their
parents have never talked with them about death, its meaning, or its sorrow.

Part of the learning that takes place in this session is practicing how to help someone who needs comfort from others.
Students practice talking to a friend who may have just lost
a father or mother or to someone who has just learned he or
she is dying. They also learn by writing notes of sympathy,
practicing how to express concern for someone who is grieving. Some have never done these things before. Students often finish this session more mature and thoughtful, better
prepared to say a final good-bye to someone at some time
whom they love—and more comfortable in helping others
do the same.

THE REWARDS—THEIRS AND YOURS

People often ask if training such as this doesn't turn
young people into arrogant, superior-acting students. I have
never seen this happen, and if it did, we would have failed
in our teaching. On the contrary, many become more modest about themselves, perhaps because they are learning
more about what human behavior, including their own, is
all about. Peer counselors do not use offices, nor are they
assigned to a "rap room" to be available for help—the kind
of things that might tend to set them apart from others.
Rather, they are taught that caring about others applies to
every circumstance of their lives with whomever they meet.
They learn that service and friendship are nice words, but
both are demanding. Even students with religious commitments have to learn the practical meaning of their faith and
what is involved in loving another as oneself.

But there are rewards! As peer counselors practice what
they learn, some see the effect this has on themselves, and
when they realize they have made a significant difference
in someone else's life—a gift that no one can take away—
the reward is priceless! When the realization hits, their faces

explode with joy—and a deep satisfaction enters their inner selves. You can't feel like a zero when this happens.

Adults experience these rewards, too. If they didn't, many of our leaders who have volunteered their services, some as many as six years of doing this after their regular jobs, wouldn't be involved. A student once said, "Peer counseling is like taking a good bath once a week." A teacher who was a leader of an after-school group said, "Peer counseling is the one thing that puts me back together each week." I have learned more, felt more effective, and received greater satisfaction from my work in peer counseling than from any other professional work I have done. Others have experienced the impact of this program on their lives also.

Warren knew he was neither a dynamo as a school teacher nor a social success in groups. But when a peer counseling leadership training was offered in another part of the state, he decided to go as a way of getting a vacation. He planned to stay only two of the five days and then take off for skiing. He ended up staying the whole week. He returned to his school and shortly afterward began a peer counseling class for some of his students. His attitude and behavior changed toward his work and those around him. Eventually he went to graduate school to get his masters degree in counseling so he could be even more effective in teaching these skills to his students.

Young people have shown they want, and can make a commitment to fight for, a more caring, less lonely world. They have proven they can be a valuable human resource in the prevention of many of the emotional wounds of adolescence. They have also contributed to the self-esteem of their peers—something that is often difficult for adults to do, even those in professional roles. Few come to the program with caring motives or a great deal of knowledge of what caring is all about. But many leave with a genuine yet humble respect for themselves and concern for others. What individual students do may seem like a teardrop in the ocean of hurts that are all around us, but a collection of such tears in a school, church, hospital, or community can create a wave that spreads and moves on.

More needs to be done so that everyone, young and old, can feel the effects of real friendship and learn how they, too, can become the friend they want for themselves. Whenever we participate in achieving this, we become one of the givers of the priceless gift of love.

Acknowledgments

No one writes a book without the significant help of many people, nor is an educational program developed independent of the contributions of others. Throughout the writing of this book and the development of the Peer Counseling Program I have been aided, supported, and constructively encouraged by many *real friends*. Without them my writing goal would not have been reached. Dr. C. Gilbert Wrenn, my consulting editor, had the major role in shaping the quality and content of the book. A beloved mentor, counselor, and friend, he also provided endless encouragement and prodding. Pamela Boyers Toole and James C. Toole are my co-workers and assistant developers of the Peer Counseling Program as it exists today. They demonstrate in countless ways the living meaning of being a real friend. Dottie Canoose typed and retyped the final manuscript, with patience and love. Similar help was given by Lorna Loungway, who typed early versions of the manuscript. My husband, Vernon, listened, read, encouraged, exercised patience, and endured the long hours I devoted to completing my goal. Thank you all for your priceless gifts of friendship and love.

The significant message of *Real Friends* has been written by young people—the peer counselors themselves. Many have given me the privilege of sharing their words and actions with you. Some helped in critical reviews of the manuscript. Thank you: Allen Briskin, Tammi Canoose, Harriet Coulson, Linda Eisner, David Ernst, Carrie Fitzpatrick, Janet Fox, Stephanie Funk, Elizabeth Gioumousis, Ned Harwood, Nathan Hessler, Brenda Huschka, Oni Kriegler, Barbara Cohn Liepman, Annette Lowowski, Elisabeth Ludeman, Gloria Moskowitz, Diane Oakley, Elke Pokorney, Scott Robinson, Dori Rose, Lisa Sabbag, Mike Shroyer, Mimi Stuart, and Shawna Westly.

Books on Counseling and Human Relations

Adler, Ronald, and Towne, Neil. *Looking Out/Looking In.* New York: Holt, Rinehart and Winston, 1981.

Brammer, Lawrence. *The Helping Relationship: Process and Skills.* Englewood Cliffs, N.J.: Prentice-Hall, 1973.

Danish, Steven, and Hauer, Allen. *Helping Skills: A Basic Training Program.* New York: Behavioral Publications, 1973.

D'Augelli, Anthony; D'Augelli, Judith; and Danish, Steven. *Helping Others.* Monterey Cal.: Brooks/Cole, 1981.

Fletcher, Kenneth; Norem-Hebeisen, Ardyth; Johnson, David; and Underwager, Ralph. *Extend: Youth Reaching Youth.* Minneapolis: Augsburg Publishing House, 1974.

Goldstein, Arnold; Sprafkin, Robert; Gershaw, N. Jane; and Klein, Paul. *Skill-Streaming the Adolescent.* Champaign, Ill.: Research Press, 1980.

Hebeisen, Ardyth. *Peer Program for Youth.* Minneapolis: Augsburg Publishing House, 1973.

Johnson, David. *Reaching Out.* Englewood Cliffs, N.J.: Prentice-Hall, 1972.

Miller, William. *Big Kids' Mother Goose.* Minneapolis: Augsburg Publishing House, 1976.

Schwarzrock, Shirley, and Wrenn, C. Gilbert. *The Coping with Series.* Circle Pines, Minn.: American Guidance Service, 1973

Schwarzrock, Shirley, and Wrenn, C. Gilbert. *Contemporary Concerns of Youth*. Circle Pines, Minn.: American Guidance Service, 1979.

Welter, Paul. *How to Help a Friend*. Wheaton, Ill.: Tyndale House Publishers, 1978.

Index

Adolescence: bumps of, 5–6; handicaps of, 6–18
Adults, importance of, 11
Alcohol, use in search of happiness, 131–132
Aloof mask, 26–27

Balancing the account, gamble of, 131
Barclay, William, 17, 18
Body, using, in welcoming, 85–86, 90
Bodyguard mask, 27–28
Body language, 65–67
Bombeck, Erma, 57
Boyers, Pam, 183
Bridging the Gap, 7
Bumps of adolescence, 5–6

Caring: commitment of, 133–134; compared to responsibility, 10
Carson, Johnny, 41, 43
Cipher in the Snow, 9
Clique mask, 27–28
Cliques, 13–14, 28
Closed door handicap of adolescence, 7, 15–18
Closed-ended question, 45–50
Clown mask, 27
Commitments, gambles of, 132–134
Conversation, beginning, 21–39; basic skills, 30–36, 38–39;

sincerity, importance of, 33, 36–37; masks, and taking them off, 23–29
Counseling, defined, 93–94, 101–102
Curriculum, of Peer Counseling Program, 186–189
Curriculum Guide for Student Peer Counseling Training, 186

Daily Celebration, 17
Death, 141–161; as cause of grief, 148–153; experiences with, 145–148; how to help, 153–159; suicide, 159–161; thinking about, 144–145
Death: The Final Stage of Growth, 142
Directions, giving, in welcoming, 87, 90
Distractor mask, 27
Drugs, use in search of happiness, 131–132

Escape, gamble of, 130–131
Escape mask, 25–26

Failure to help, 111–112
Fathers, time spent with, 12
Feelings, listening for, 63–65
Filter, listening, 58–62
The Five Cries of Youth, 14, 16, 17, 38, 74, 80, 82, 83, 90

Food, use to welcome, 84–85, 90
Francis of Assisi, 133
Frankl, Viktor, 134
"Free information," using in
    conversation, 31–32
Full-time pleasure, gamble of,
    129–130
Funeral, vs. memorial service,
    155–156

Gambles of commitments, 132–134
Gambles of finding happiness,
    129–132
Good Samaritan, 112–114
Grief, causes of, 148–153
Group, welcoming into a, 76–91

Hamburg, Dr. Beatrix, viii
Handicaps of adolescence, 6–18;
    closed door, 7, 15–18; problem-
    prone image, 6, 7–10; separate
    worlds, 7, 10–15
Happiness, gambles of finding,
    129–132
Healing, 111. See also Helping
Hello, saying, 21–39; basic skills,
    30–36, 38–39; masks, and taking
    them off, 23–29; sincerity,
    importance of, 33, 36–37
Helping, 93–114; after a death,
    153–159; answers to give,
    102–111; example, 112–114;
    failure, 111–112; qualities of
    helper, 95–97; rating yourself,
    97–99
Honesty. See Sincerity and honesty

Image, negative, changing, 8–9
Informational question, 45–50
Interviewing, avoiding: in
    conversation, 32; in welcoming,
    86–87, 90
Introducing yourself, 31
"It's gotta be me," gamble of, 130

Jesus, x, 111

Konopka, Gisela, 118
Kübler-Ross, Elisabeth, 142

Life: using as price of admission,
    gamble of, 131–132; value of,
    128–129
Listening, 32, 55–69; after a death,
    156–157; body language, 65–67;
    clarifying meanings of words,
    62–63; listening for feelings,
    63–65; practicing, 67–69; your
    listening filter, 58–62
Loneliness, after a death, 157–159
Love, commitment of, 133–134

Masks, 23–29; aloof or put-down
    mask, 26–27; clique mask, 27–28;
    clown or distractor mask, 27;
    escape mask, 25–26; taking off,
    28–29
Meanings of words, clarifying, 62–63
Memorial service, vs. funeral,
    155–156
Millard, Cherie A., 118
Mizer, Jean, 3
Models, adults as, 11

Open-ended question, 45–50

Peer Counseling Program, 181–191;
    beginnings of, viii–ix; curriculum
    of, 186–189; explanation of,
    18–19, 38–39; framework of,
    183–186; philosophy of, 182–183;
    rewards and results of, 163–178,
    189–191
Peer Counseling Recognition
    Dinner, 163
Personal question, 45–50
Personnel, of Peer Counseling
    Program, 183–184

The Phantom Tollbooth, 109
"Please Hear What I'm Not
    Saying," 106
Powell, John, 119, 129, 130
Privacy, respecting, in conversation,
    33–34
Problem-prone image handicap of
    adolescence, 6, 7–10
Put-down mask, 26–27

Questions, asking, 41–52; closed-
    ended, 45–50; informational,
    45–50; open-ended, 45–50;
    personal, 45–50; problems with,
    43–45; sincerity, importance of,
    50–52

Regret, in grief, 150
Rescuing, in welcoming, 87–88, 90
Responsibility, compared to caring,
    10
Rewards and results, of Peer
    Counseling Program, 163–178,
    189–191

Scala, Dr. Michael, 142
Schedules, of Peer Counseling
    Program, 184–186
Separate worlds handicap of
    adolescence, 7, 10–15
Shakespeare, William, 178
Sincerity and honesty, importance
    of: after a death, 154–155; in

asking questions, 50–52; in
    beginning a conversation, 33,
    36–37
Solutions, helping one find, 110–111
Strommen, Merton, 7, 14, 16, 83
Suicide, 159–161; preventing, 160;
    reasons for, 159–160
Sympathy, compared to counseling,
    101–102

Toole, James, 183

Unconditional Love, 129, 130
Useful purpose, commitment to,
    132–133

Values, finding your, 117–138; the
    future, 125–128; gambles of
    commitment, 132–134; gambles of
    finding happiness, 129–132; the
    past, 120–123; personal rating,
    136–138; the present, 123–125;
    value of life, 128–129

Welcome: into a group, 76–91;
    meaning of, 79; return for, 89–90
*Why Am I Afraid to Tell You Who
    I Am?* 119
Wrenn, Gilbert, 106
Wrenn, Dr. Robert, 142

Young Girls, 118